A Phoenix Rising

Defining the Moments

Bryan Nash

Bryan Nash Publications, LLC

Orange, CA

A Phoenix Rising: Defining the Moments

Cover design by Robert Gould

ISBN: 978-0-9797604-0-2

Library of Congress Control Number: 2007905330

Published by Bryan Nash Publications, LLC.

1744 W. Katella Ave., Suite #100

Orange, CA 92867

Printed and bound in the United States of America

To My Children:

    To my son Ryan, who gave me the childhood I never had, whose spirit lives on within so many whom he touched in the few moments that he shared.

    To my daughter Lauren, who gives me the opportunity to be a good father, someone to look up to and someone to be proud of.

I Love You Both

Author's Notes

As a survivor of an abusive childhood I found myself sharing stories of the many events that filled and impacted my early years. As friends and acquaintances both new and old listened to me, I observed their expressions. Most were amazed, many were stunned but not one ever doubted my words, for they knew, as anyone would, these were words that could only come from someone who lived these types of experiences.

So, to fulfill the many requests and the several promises, I have put these words to paper in hopes to enlighten some and encourage others that still struggle within the circumstances of their life's path.

The complexity of my experiences made difficult the task of presenting this work in a way that would answer questions as it unfolded and evolved into my passage toward safety.

After pondering this dilemma from all imaginable angles, the simplest solution seemed to appear from nowhere. Awakening in the wee hours of the morning, the answer came to mind: this story can only be told in three parts.

Part I

I opted to write this opening section of my work in a third person format. The stories are enchanting and read like fairy tales as they are the memories of my older sister as told to me. This is only fitting, for without her input I would not have understood the obscured memories I recalled from those first few years of my life. These years are the cornerstones that support my faith in God, for without these blessings, I would be somebody else.

Part II

In this part of the book, the narrative is switched to first person as these are the stories of which I have independent memory. They cover the ten years my sister and I spent together enduring outrageous acts of abuse, leaving us with physical, mental, and emotional distress.

Part III

In this section, I share the final four years, spent alone, after my sister came of age and escaped our hell. Left behind, I found a way to cope, deal with and overcome the circumstances before me.

With my path taking its final radical twist, and through the influences of others, I find the ability to grasp empowerment with a rare and comprehensive insight. Learning to seek only peace of mind, my strategic exodus unfolds as I turn the tables of abusive oppression, taking with me an incredible story of survival, triumph and enlightenment we all can learn from.

Rising from the ashes, I surface with my spirit intact.

Preface

What I really would like to say…

Several years ago, as a young man I emerged from the confining trials of life as a foster child. The situational dynamics were not so unique, as many children faced with abandonment eventually find themselves taken in by relatives, as did my sister and I.

What is unique is our path: the journey through a time before child services recognized the significant difference between child discipline and child abuse. A time when ill intent could capitalize on innocence and the authorities looked the other way. A time before a teacher dared to ask a child about life at home or bruises on their body. A time before a neighbor dared to pick up the phone and call the police.

This is the story of two orphans who learned love's blessings on a working farm in Cedartown, Georgia. A story about a brief stay in an enchanted place where, at the end of the day, an old woman rocked in her chair and read Bible stories to a dozen little souls with listening ears, unselfishly teaching good from evil and that God will always be near.

It's about the impact of an advantageous aunt who worked the system from both ends to supplement her income while her home was kept up by child labor. Ruled by a heavy hand, two orphans walked the line inside the walls of another family's home, their roles defined by the daily routine, servants who worked to earn their keep.

This is the story of my sister's pain, a heart torn by the absence of a mother she knew until she was four; a mother she knew would, one day, return; a mother I never knew, but through the lonely dark void in my sister's eyes.

It's the story of my pain as I was held back, helpless, seeing her beaten bloody. It's about my confusion as we ran, with my hand in hers, until caught by the police and returned to their custody.

It's about survival, endurance and toleration through circumstances and situations; it's about mindset and interpretation, tenacity and tactics.

But, most of all, this is a story about love; the love of my sister; the love we learned from the old woman on the farm; the love we lacked inside the walls of that house and the love that found us outside of that house. This story is about the love from the many angels that helped me through, showing me the vision of hope that lay beyond my circumstances in the treacherous floor of the forest concealing my path from the world outside.

This story is for all…

To the many...

...that have blessed my life at the most amazing times, illuminating the shadowy bends twisting before the steps in my path.

To my sister Cindy and her brave sacrifice, stepping in front to protect me. For standing strong through the adversity; and sharing her beautiful voice that uplifted me during a difficult time in my life. For her faith in Daddy-God - our God - the one to whom she spoke when praying at the top of that tree.

To my three amigos: Jimmy Gastelo, Rick Jones, and Simon Gomez. Like brothers they always are there, bringing clarity to my life in the streets and understanding to the dynamics we faced growing up in a most interesting and important place in time.

To my mentor - my "Mom" - Nellie Kaniski, she is the lady next door that sent me love as a child. She is the angel in my life that taught me to lead with my heart.

To my God Parents, the Lucios; and the other angels that gave me encouragement through their touch or their subtle gaze, helping me through just knowing that they were aware and they cared.

There are so many, some still here and others who wait patiently on the other side for my work to be done. To all of you, I say thank you for being there.

Forgiveness

This work was not written with a vindictive heart; it is simply a true story in which names were NOT changed to protect the perpetrators. It is a reminder that abuse hides behind lies and oppression, deceit and indiscretions that manipulate our children, changing their lives forever.

To those who have suffered at the hands of another, there is freedom in forgiveness. Remember — there is no reward in hurting someone else.

To those who have endured, I say step forward, speak out, and never give up an opportunity to reach out, for your gesture in that moment may truly make a difference.

Teach your children well.

A Phoenix Rising

Defining the Moments

Bryan Nash

In my crib, left for hours, hungry, I cry aloud. My bottom burns from a soiled diaper. My mother is nowhere near, but I am not alone: my first spiritual visitor has just arrived.

Clouds that Ground

Early Spring, 1957

"Slam!" goes the wooden screen door a split second after squeezing past the narrow gap made from all her efforts, counteracting the spring hinges it hangs by. Barely a foot or so open, it's just enough for her to escape from the heat of the small wooden house. After slipping out, she tippy-toes softly, avoiding any splinters along the way till she finds herself at the steps of the old wooden porch.

Perched near the edge, she settles down, resting her feet upon the second step. Now, her eyes wander about until they come to rest on the tractor tire that hangs from a knotted rope looped about and fastened to a large branch of oak. It's that branch that has all of her attention and desire.

Standing on the top of that big tire she can reach to the third knot, but she hasn't the strength to pull herself up as her arms are still too small.

Today, she will opt for the limbs of the willow, as it grows nearly horizontal to the ground. Off she runs, through the grass field that covers the gentle sloping way. It's but a moment, and she hears Melody calling out, "Cindy! Cindy! Wait for me!"

Standing on a boulder, the tip that has breached the low waters of the pond, she waits for the little Asian girl with pigtails to catch up. Together, they laugh at the funny little fishy-frogs that scoot across the moss covered bottom, hiding beneath a pond lily. Seconds later they lose count of how many, for they are out of fingers and know only up to ten.

~.~.~.~

Northern Georgia is known for some brutal weather this time of year. The rainstorms are plenty and the thunderbolts leave scars across the sky that fill themselves with amazing pastels of orange and red. The forest that's not so far away begins to turn obscure as clouds slip in from afar. Not long after, the sun dims and the mugginess of the afternoon sets in.

Cloud-to-ground storms are a normal occurrence and the stories go back generations how these vessels of smoked white carry large strikes of lightning that illuminate the horizons in the darkest of nights. Soon, the cracks of thunder begin much closer this time, sending the two little girls running for shelter. Along the way, the sprinkles began. *So what*, they think, *getting soaked just means an early bath.*

"I'll race you, smarty pants," yells Cindy, taking off and outrunning Melody's reply. Of course she won't keep up and Cindy, like a driven wind, flies toward home, leaving her dark skinned, amber eyed little friend far behind.

Nearing the barn on the far side of the house, she cuts across the path that runs along the flowering peas and through the dirt yard where chickens scatter. She's headed for that tire under the oak. As though she is outrunning the lightning, her feet rhythmically patter along without missing a beat.

"CRACK-BOOM!" sounds the lightning as she nears the shelter of the tree, she stops and looks back to see where smarty pants might be. There she was, just rounding the edge of the barn. A sigh of relief escapes Cindy's lips and she sits on the tire for a second waiting for her best friend to catch up. It's then that another large "CRACK-BOOM!" follows and Melody freezes in her tracks. Cindy lay still beneath the large oak, frozen, her face in mud, the smell of burnt rope lingering nearby.

The oak had been hit by a large thunderbolt. The tractor tire lay flat on its side next to Cindy. Just a second had lapsed before Melody screams "Cindyyyyyyy!" screeching the activities inside the farmhouse to an abrupt halt. Mama Skinner stands in the doorway, canvassing the scene.

Within moments, the old woman is scooping the little girl into her arms and heading for the steps. Inside, on the eating table, she lays Cindy as Melody brings a pail of water. The other children, orphans they are, gather about. Just like Cindy, most have been abandoned somewhere at sometime. Minutes, several at least, go by before there is a stir. Soon, however, the little girl is asking, "What happened?"

"It's a miracle you weren't killed," says the old woman as she continues to wipe Cindy's face. "You've been hit by lightning, or at least the tree you were under was. The rope burnt to a crisp. God was looking out for you."

Once Cindy was able to stand, Mama Skinner told all the children to sit by her rocker so she could read to them. The old woman seated herself as they gathered, head bowed, and began as she always did: with a prayer. The children in their obedient way listened close as she thanked the Lord for looking out for them and protecting Cindy from harm.

Late Spring, 1958

"Hi Daddy – God,

I know You're listening, I can feel You inside me. It's Cindy. I'm here in the tree again: I climbed as high as I can, just so I can be close to You. I've been so afraid. My mommy didn't come back like she said she would. I don't know why.

Please stay close to me. You always told me You'd stay close to me 'cuz I'm so alone. Mama Skinner says it's good to talk to You and it makes me feel better when I do. Now let me sing my song to You:

Jesus loves me, this I know, 'cuz the Bible tells me so, little ones for Him be strong, they are weak so He is strong! Yes, Jesus loves me…"

Climbing from the tree, Cindy felt the rising breeze pushing the branches about, raindrops from the drizzle that began only moments before running down her face. Continuing her decent, she rushed, becoming soaked, clinging to what she could, finally reaching the large branch where the rope swing was tied. Down she scurried, like a small wet mouse, until her feet rested on top of the old tractor tire fastened to the other end of the rope. Off she hopped onto the dirt path leading to the porch.

Cindy stood on the porch, pondering the weather change that seemed to come out of nowhere. This wasn't the first time strange things happened when she climbed that tree. Somehow, deep inside, she felt there was more to this sudden downpour. It would be just a few weeks later that she would know that her talk with Daddy-God would be answered in the most amazing way.

Warm showers were common for spring and the little farm in Cedartown flourished as crops blossomed on the rolling hills leading up to the orchards near the forest. Papa Lue came chugging up the road with baskets of apples, freshly picked and loaded in the bed of his beat up truck. Mamma Skinner was out on the porch with news that Cindy's mother was gonna be stopping by just for a bit.

"Papa, you'll need to send little Cindy on back 'cuz her mama's a come calling. Says she got a surprise for her."

"Yessum," answered her husband of thirty-some-odd years. This was their third year trying to make this farm earn a living and it took every bit of daylight and many a prayer answered to make ends meat.

It wasn't long thereafter that Cindy came down from the orchards, leading Charlie by his bridle, the wagon filled with baskets of more red apples. Charlie was a gentle ole gelding, with just a bit of work left in him. If it wasn't for that wagon he still pulled, he would have been off to the glue factory. These poor folks couldn't keep anything that wasn't paying its own way.

"Hurry on up now, Cindy, lest your mamma's gonna see you with your hair brushed and your feet washed up," Mamma Skinner calls out. Under her breath she mumbles, "Sure hope she's bringing some money. Can't keep going on nothing; it's been months now without a dime."

Cindy has no idea why her mother is suddenly coming to visit but is excited just the same. "Mamma Skinner, can you read to me before my mother gets here?"

"Well now dear, let's get cleaned up first and let me get them pies out the stove and, if your mamma ain't here by then, I'll be happy to read from the Bible whatever you'd like."

"I'll be ready right quick," says Cindy and she scurries on out with a pail to pump some fresh water.

Cindy sat quietly on the floor next to Mamma Skinner while the old lady rocked methodically in her chair, reading scripture in the most proper way. This was a treat, as all the other children on the farm were still up in the orchards. Seldom did any of them get read to during the day, for this was special, reserved for the evening after supper and before bedtime.

For some reason, the two of them had a special bond that had formed over the last two years Cindy had been on the farm. Mamma Skinner was never blessed with children of her own and she treated Cindy in a special way; but still, Cindy longed for and missed her mother deeply, never really understanding why she was sent away in the first place. All she remembered was being touched in places that were private and being scared of the man that always burned spiders with a match. In a blink, she found herself far from what she knew to be her home in sunny South Miami. When her mommy dropped her off she said she would be back soon but Christmas has come by twice since then and she hasn't heard a word.

People talked a whole lot different here than they did back home. The sun came out early and when it went down it was time for all the children to step in the metal tub and wash off. In from one side and out the other; each one would sit down briefly and be dried off as they stepped out. Once dressed for bed, they would take their place at the feet of the old woman in the rocker and listen to her read from the Bible.

Many things were different. Back home, she would be wakened by loud voices in the middle of the night. That's when her mommy would come home from work. She smelled and sounded different than she did when she left, but it was always the same after she came home from work. Had Cindy known what alcohol was then, she would have known that her mother had a disease that was self-inflicted at the club where she worked. Sometimes, Cindy would go with her if the lady next door didn't wake up.

Her mother referred to the lady as an alcoholic, whatever that meant. She was happy just going to work with her mommy and staying in her little room until she fell asleep.

Many times late at night she would wake up to the heavy voices of men talking. Creeping from her bed, Cindy peeked though the keyhole in her door to see several men sitting around the living room, smoking cigarettes and drinking an amber colored liquid from a bottle they passed about. Their voices were low, as if they were telling secrets out loud, and they always seemed to address her mommy's boyfriend, Uncle Louie, as "Boss." He *was* the boss, her mommy said, and he talked business in the wee hours of the morning with the same men every time. Uncle Louie always had a gun with him and so did the other men when they visited, but mommy said he wasn't a policeman.

When Mamma Skinner finished reading to Cindy, they went into the kitchen and started peeling potatoes for supper. Each afternoon, Cindy helped her as she was one of the oldest children at the age of five-and-a-half. As the potatoes would fall peeled into the tub – the same tub that they bathed in – Cindy would take the brush and scrub them clean before putting them back on the rough wooden counter.

After they finished washing the potatoes, they carried the tub out to the porch just in time to see a big cloud of dust forming out yonder near the bend in the road. Papa Lue came running from the hay barn, waving his hat and yelling, "Slow down, gosh darn it!"

As the big sedan came to a halt, the cloud of dust caught up to and covered them entirely. But when the dust cleared and the doors opened, out stepped the most beautiful lady Cindy had ever seen. She looked like a movie star and she was carrying something, a bundle wrapped in blankets and a bag that dangled off her forearm. As she walked forward in her high heels, gracefully navigating the uneven dirt path, Cindy knew that it was her mother and yet, as much as she missed her, she froze in amazement, waiting for her at the porch.

"Hi Ginger, how you been?" asked Mama Skinner.

"Things are getting better," she replied. "Louie's in jail and I just can't get anything done with a newborn – there's money in the bag."

As she hands the bag to Mama Skinner she reaches down and gives Cindy a hug. Cindy holds on tight, but at the same time feels like she is hugging a stranger. If not for the familiar scent of alcohol, the feel was totally different. It's been over two years and she seems nothing like the woman she remembers.

"Here honey, this is your new baby brother." As she hands the bundle to Cindy she says, "His name is Eddie."

Early Summer, 1958

"Daddy-God

Thank You for sending my mommy to me and bringing my new baby brother. I am no longer lonely! I am happy Daddy-God!

My little Eddie is here with me and he needs me to take care of him. He is so tiny! I change his diapers - Mama Skinner showed me how. I hold him and Mama Skinner lets me sit in her rocking chair so's I can rock him and soothe him to sleep.

Daddy-God, You have answered my prayers. You have blessed me with my new little brother."

As Cindy looked to the sky, through the leaves of the tree far out in the horizon she saw the most amazing thing. As far as she could see, brilliant shades of green, yellow, orange and blue arched across the cloudless sky. *What's that?* she thought to herself as she scampered down from the tree. Holding onto the rope, knot by knot, she lowered herself down till she could leap to the ground below.

"Mama Skinner! Mama Skinner!" she yelled out. Soon, from the chicken coupe, came the old woman that had the answers to her question.

"Yes dear, what is it?" she asked.

"Mama Skinner, what is that?" and she pointed to the sky.

"Oh Cindy, that is a sign from the Lord! God speaks to us in amazing ways, and that is what's called a rainbow."

That night, after everyone was bathed and ready for bed, they all gathered near the rocking chair to hear the old woman read. When the Bible was opened, the story shared with the children was about a man named Noah and his ark.

That evening the children learned about the pairs of animals that went two-by-two into the ark so they wouldn't drown from the Great Flood that was coming. God needed to cleanse the Earth because of all the evil that had spoiled the land and, by flooding the Earth, the land would be cleansed. When He was finished He sent a great sign to all that survived and that sign was the rainbow. Through the rainbow, all would know that God was near, for it could be seen from everywhere.

As she lay in her bunk in the room with twelve other kids, Cindy thought about the events of the day and again about how the rainbow appeared after she talked to Daddy-God. There was never a doubt that He heard her prayers and that He spoke to her through His signs. First, the down pour a few weeks back and now the rainbow. She truly knew that her every word had been heard. As she closed her eyes she prayed,

"Daddy-God,

Now I lay me down to sleep; I pray to You my soul to keep; should I die before I wake; I pray that my soul You will take. Bless my mommy and my Mamma Skinner and Papa Lue and my baby brother, Eddie, and all the children on the farm and Charlie too."

Late Summer, 1958

In no time at all her little brother was crawling about and entertaining himself with corn cobs and whittled sticks from Papa Lue. Eddie was full of adventure and began walking at a very young age. Pulling himself up along the walls and staggering across the door openings, it wasn't long before his balance kicked in and he was darting across the room.

"My, he's a quick one," said Papa Lue. It was Sunday morning and all the children either climbed or were loaded into the back of the old truck to go to worship and give praise to the Lord. Little Eddie was on Cindy's lap as they bounced about and rolled down the old dirt road. Sunday school was never missed, even if you were dying. If you were sick you sat on the bench outside of the window and listened in. Eddie squirmed a lot and, when he became a distraction, Cindy would have to take him to the bench so he wouldn't get them in trouble.

In the chapel, all the grown ups would be singing halleluiah and raising their hands to the sky. What a sight to see if you have never been to a Southern Baptist Church. Religion was a big part of life in North-Western Georgia and most everyone participated. Today was special, as Cindy was going to be baptized down in the pond.

After worship, all the people filed out of the church as they sung and clapped their hands while marching toward the pond. No sooner would one song end than another would begin with the preacher singing out "Praise the Lord!" as the women swayed side to side, continuing their walk to the "Holy Water."

They would gather near the banks as the preacher waded his way to the center of the pond, raising his hands and calling to the Lord. Cindy worked her way out to him as all looked upon this very holy moment. The Mulberry brush was tall on the backside of the pond so everyone crowded the front edge where they could see, placing their bare feet into the cool water. With words of grace, he offered her to the Lord and dunked her well under the surface. When she emerged, she came up spitting and choking, crying from the ordeal but baptized nonetheless.

The Blue Raven

Late Autumn, 1958

It must have been late afternoon that autumn day because Cindy had just returned from the orchards, leading Charlie toward the barn with a wagon full of apples.

She instinctively scanned the road up ahead for her little brother who had stayed behind at the farmhouse. The day was a bit too crisp for him or his best little friend Popie to be out. Popie had a chronic runny nose and seemed to be on the sickly side for a two year old. Since he arrived at the orphanage a few months back, he had been to the hospital twice with pneumonia.

Still looking for a sign of Eddie, she led Charlie into the barn and up to the hay bin where she tossed in a flake of hay to occupy him till Papa Lue arrived. Cindy approached the old farmhouse, peeking under the porch briefly just in case Eddie was hiding there. He had many places he liked to hide and, being so small, he could crawl into the tightest nooks. Not seeing him, she went inside where she found Popie bundled up in a blanket near the wood burning stove keeping warm.

"Afternoon there, my beautiful Cindy," said Mama Skinner.

"Have you seen my baby?" Cindy replied.

"He was playing on the porch just a spell back. Best go check the chicken coupe, honey."

As Cindy walked out to the porch, the coolness in the air brought a brief shiver to her so she buttoned her raggedy blue coat and wrapped her arms to her chest.

Passing under the big oak where the tire swing hung, an odd feeling came over her and she froze. Somehow, she knew Eddie was not in the chicken coup. Still, she checked inside.

Just last month, she found him literally crawled up inside one of the cages. Papa Lue was not so happy about that and it took a lot of scrubbing to get that mess off him. Eddie's feet were so tiny he could wrap his toes around the little cleats on the wooden planks just like the chickens would and walk up to the feeding trough where his bare feet could trounce through the grain.

Now where? she wondered and walked around the backside of the barn where the pea patch grew. Down onto her hands and knees she went to look through the cracks in the siding of an old shed. She found him there not so long ago. He just squeezed past a broken board, catching his knee on a bent rusty nail in the process.

"Not there," she said to herself and then, off like the wind, she ran to the pig pens. "He better not be near that mama sow, she'd just sit on him. Where is he?" She asked herself as she turned and headed for the farm-house again.

"Mama Skinner, I can't find him and it's getting dark."

By now, the rest of the children were back from the orchards and joined in the search. Looking up, Cindy saw Billy, one of the older boys, standing in the doorway of the hay loft shrugging his shoulders. The children began to fan out and call for him as they canvassed the farm. There were a million places he could be hiding, including the gullies and bushes, the corn field and who knows where else? Cindy was getting scared and she began to cry.

Desperately, Cindy climbs up the rope swing, pulling herself by the large knots that will lead her to the branch upon which she can hoist herself. Crawling through the branches, she keeps her eyes looking about, hoping to get a glimpse, but there is nothing. Continuing as high as she can, her mind now goes to the reason she climbed the tree in the first place. With tears rolling off her cheeks, her trembling little palms come together and she begins to pray,

"Daddy – God,

> **Please help me find my baby, Eddie. I can't find him anywhere and**

I'm so afraid! He is nowhere to be found, Daddy - God, and everyone is looking for him. I don't know what to do! Please, make him be safe. I couldn't live if anything happened to my baby, Eddie"

Sitting still, legs wrapped around the branch that supported her, Cindy feels the same brief shiver she felt earlier on the porch. Pulling her hands to her chest, she sees a large raven flying overhead nearly into the tree itself. Calling out, the large bird seems to be telling Cindy something, but what? Out of nowhere this bird comes nearly crashing into her, screeching loudly. Now circling above, the raven has captured Cindy's full attention and she calls out "what, what?!" as if she knows it is a sign from her **Daddy-God.**

Instinctively, Cindy begins to climb down from the tree. Quickly, she finds the rope and nearly flies to the ground while the raven continues to hover. Waiting for her to appear from under the large oak canopy, the magical bird calls to her, telling her to follow.

Sure enough, Cindy peeks to the sky and the raven flies far out ahead and then back toward her as she runs in its direction. The other children soon take notice and they stare as Cindy continues to run, crossing a field and cutting through an old path that is barely visible through the tall weeds and mulberry bush. The bird continues on quite far and then back to a point, circling before coming to rest atop a dead cedar tree near the wash.

Seldom has Cindy been over to this side of the farm land – once, maybe, looking for berries near the stream last summer.

Nearing the stump, the raven again calls out to her but stays put, squawking in the early twilight, surrounding Cindy as she stands. There is a calm stillness and the raven is now silhouetted by the backdrop of a crescent moon, but the sky is still alive with an energy of sorts, making the moment nearly sacred.

"Why have you brought me here? Where is my baby, Eddie?" she asks and, like an angel, the large bird jumps off the old hollow and glides to the edge of the path and her question is answered.

There, below the edge of the path at the cut of the wash, is an irrigation pipe tunneling under the slope and coming out several yards away. Her eyes widen as Cindy realizes **Daddy - God** has once again answered her prayer. Just inside, out of sight sat her baby, Eddie, playing with some worms he had found in the wash. Quickly, she gathers him into her arms as the other children reach her and stare at the magical bird in front of the moon that has, once again, perched itself on the hollow. Behind the children stood Mama Skinner holding Popie in her arms with an amazed look on her face.

As they walked back to the old farmhouse, no one uttered a word. All remained quiet except for Mama Skinner who had just witnessed the bizarre behavior of the largest raven she had ever seen. She spoke to the children in terms of miracles and signs from the Lord above and assured the children that they had all just witnessed exactly that: a miracle from God. When she finished talking the children called out, "It's raining! It's raining!" as large, but infrequent drops sprinkled lightly.

Cindy looked up at Mama Skinner and said, "***Daddy - God*** hears you. Can you feel His happy tears? He is telling you so with His rain drops."

Enchanted Land

As with many parts of the south, Cedartown was as rich in history as was the soil beneath the crops and trees that thrived. Known as the "Valley of the Cedars," its land was fertile and dotted with large groves of aromatic trees and long leaf Pines. The Creek Indians referred to the area as "Big Springs" before it was overtaken by the Cherokee after the Creek's loss at the Taliwa tribal games. Cherokee Nation now expanded south to "Beaver Dam" that lies on Cedar Creek, just west of the spring in what is now known as Cedar Town, Georgia – the county seat of Polk.

Much of our country's folklore has been generated from this area including "The Trail of Tears," and its legacy, the "Cherokee Rose," that remains Georgia's state flower. Over four thousand souls, one for every quarter mile, left their earthly bodies along this trail, joining the great "Spirit in the Sky," departing what some know as the "Enchanted Land."

And so we wondered, after the Blue Raven led Cindy to her brother, just how sacred her connection to **Daddy-God** really was. Whenever she was in the tree, it seemed she could speak to Him and have her words be heard. But it wasn't just the tree that seemed mystical. The entire *farm* had this energy about it, as if there were some magical power that kept us feeling close to a very spiritual place.

Maybe it was Mama Skinner and her strong faith that influenced us; or perhaps it was the environment she created. Although we were no doubt a poor farm struggling to get by, we always seemed to make it to the next season's crop planting and the hand-harvest that soon followed. The Blue Raven became elusive and, although talked about often, we never saw him again. Mama Skinner never let us forget that what happened that day was divine. An intervention. A miracle.

Summer, 1959

The following summer, another amazing sign from ***Daddy - God*** came, resulting from an incident that would take place near a bend in the road, just past the old wooden bridge that crossed over the creek bed. It was a somber afternoon and the children on the farm were returning from the Independence Day picnic held down at the old church. The air seemed to move slowly as it radiated heat across the wheat fields that bordered the road leading back to the farmhouse. Earlier that year, the spring showers left the dirt road rutted, with many stones exposed, making the walk that much more difficult on our bare feet.

Eddie was lagging as his little legs didn't cover much ground, making it hard to keep up with the older kids that ran ahead. Cindy called out to one of the boys to hurry back with the bicycle so's they could give him a ride.

Soon enough, Billy came bouncing on up with the old rusty bike. The large balloon tires with white sidewalls were worn bald but still held air long enough to last a day. On the front, a rusty old basket was fastened to the handlebars by bailing wire, and a tin horn with a red rubber ball dangled from its side. Cindy picked her little brother up and placed him side-saddle on the back fender running behind as Billy peddled off. With his hands in the air, Eddie balanced himself as they bounced along, headed for the bridge. With his tiny britches rolled in a cuff just under his knees and sporting a small straw hat, he looked like a miniature Huckleberry Finn, minus the pipe.

No one could have seen it coming: it had been such a fun day and their minds were still filled with the sounds from the Dixie band and the taste of cotton candy that stuck to their fingers. The burnt orange tint in the sky behind them that streaked randomly across the horizon created a wicked backdrop for what would soon occur.

Billy, anticipating the slight climb ahead, rose up out of his seat, pushing the peddles harder to make the hill. Eddie slipped about on the fender, teetering, barely maintaining his balance as they reached the bridge with Cindy just a step behind. They crested the old wooden planks and coasted down to the other side where the front tire of the bicycle found a rut and they all folded on top of each other in a heap.

Billy was ok and Cindy picked herself up, but when she reached for her brother she shrieked. Blood poured from the side of his foot that had been laid open between the spokes of the rear wheel. On the ground below was a chunk of flesh that resembled a bite out of a drumstick, cartilage and all. His ankle was shredded to the bone, his toe tip was ripped from under the nail.

Billy ran for the farmhouse, calling out for help while Cindy tried to free her brother from the underside of the bike as he sat there, dazed and scared. The blood continued to pour and his ankle remained firmly lodged between the spokes.

The porch soon filled with kids from inside that heard Billy's cry and Mama Skinner came a running as the children fell in behind her. She was a big woman and she was stout, not really built for rapid movement. Nonetheless, she ran as fast as her legs would carry her till she collapsed on the ground next to the bicycle.

Like a seasoned medic, she tore strips of cotton from the bottom of her dress, tying the first one around Eddie's leg as a tourniquet to slow the flow of blood that puddled under him. Her hands went next to the spokes, and she pulled them until they stretched enough to free his tiny ankle.

Quickly, she tossed the bicycle aside and wrapped his wounds with more strips of cloth, gathering him into her arms, cradling his little body as she hustled back to the farmhouse.

Once inside, she sat Eddie on the wooden counter dangling his legs over the edge and called for more water to pour onto the gushing wound. As the little boy faded, she began to pray aloud for more strength, wiping the sweat from her face as she did so.

"Oh Lord, be with me! Send me strength, please, and spare this little boy!"

The other children fetched buckets of water and carried them into the little house while Billy placed the large tub underneath. Clammy, shivering and pale lay the little boy on the table as the blood continued to flow.

In the tree outside the porch – where she would always go – Cindy climbed as far as she could till she found the branch she had sat upon so many times. Scared and sobbing, she held her hands together and pointed them to the sky as she looked up and began talking to *Daddy-God.*

"Daddy - God, please can you hear me? My little brother, Eddie, is hurt so very bad and he is bleeding and it won't stop. Please, Daddy - God, please help us. Please don't let him die."

Once again, that familiar chill came across her as she pleaded for help and the orange sky began shifting about. Sitting in the tree shivering, waiting, she realized that the glow from above began to illuminate the big oak around her. A mystical feeling came over her as a thin, misty air gathered in the leaves of the canopy. Looking to the farmhouse, the hazy glow moved with her gaze as if she had harnessed this transparent cloud of orange until it was surrounding the wooden clad structure.

Cindy felt the spirit within her as she climbed from the tree and slowly walked toward the porch. There lay her tiny brother on the counter, without movement. Entering barely, her frozen gaze captured the attention of the other children who were gathered about. Popie, huddled with a blanket and holding tightly to Eddie's tiny hat, rose to his feet and stared. So did the others as they stepped back from the little boy that lay motionless on the thick wooden plank. The blood had stopped and the wounds were clean, but he hadn't moved for several minutes.

He had lost so much blood, the tub below literally *filled* with red water. Mama Skinner focused on applying a cotton bandage, felt a presence and straightened tall before slowly turning to find Cindy standing in a silhouetted glow. She stared at her little baby, Eddie, her body seemingly weightless, feeling nothing but the mysterious energy that had overcome her in the tree. It was this energy that filled the room and reached to her precious little brother, raising him up to a sitting position before his eyes had even opened. When they finally did, he smiled and looked directly toward the door and into his sister's eyes.

The others in the room followed, their eyes locked on Cindy as she stood just inside the beaten threshold of the doorway, eyes wide with amazement and a radiance illuminating her like a halo of fog burning off with the early morning sun. But this was not morning and there was no fog. Something enchanting had embraced the little farmhouse once again. Seeing Cindy standing there they knew that she had spoken to **Daddy-God.**

Could it be that the many spirits from all the lives lost along that trail are the reason this little farm seemed so magical? Or was it, perhaps, the faith of innocent children looking for a miracle and listening to an old woman preach from her pulpit, being instilled with the goodness we all deserve to know? There isn't a single answer that can satisfy everyone but, just as the poem "The Never Ending Trail" states in its closing phrase,

> **"You still can hear them crying,**
> **Along The Trail Of Tears,**
> **If you listen with your heart,**
> **And not with just your ears."**

Perhaps these little orphans were not abandoned by all. It seems that small farm had many angels watching over the little souls that were there, under the care of an old woman in a rocking chair that shared her time, her place on earth, unselfishly teaching little children that God would always be near.

The Power of Prayer

Fall, 1959

Late summer had been especially dry and the heat through September left the hillsides leading to the pine forest bristling with brownish grass. From the inside of the old farmhouse, Eddie sat looking out at the parched fields that gave way to the most amazing fall foliage North Georgia had seen in some time.

Autumn leaves with multitudes of weathered tones glistened in the early morning rays. The light from the sun shining through the glass kept him occupied, as he played with the dust particles that floated about in front of his eyes and tiny hands. Like miniature flying cows, he pretended they were in a make-believe pasture, wandering about. Some of them were standing, some were grazing and others walked slowly across the plain. The few that neared the border of the small window would be herded back carefully by his little fingers to join the rest, near the center of the sunlit pane.

In the room next to the parlor where Eddie played lay his sister Cindy, wrapped tightly in a woolen blanket in the bottom bunk. The room had three sets of bunk beds, each against the walls just like the other room where the boys would sleep. The floor was barren and there was nothing that hung on the lath and broken plaster since the orphans that slept in this room were without possessions, except for the rare doll or stuffed animal donated last Christmas by the Salem Baptist Church.

Cindy had been in bed now for several days. It started out with a sore throat and then came a raging fever. Today, well, today her tongue began looking like a fat strawberry – the ones that have big white spots on them. Mamma Skinner said she would have to stay in the room by herself the whole day.

Slipping into the hall, Eddie crept around the corner to the girls' bedroom door where he knelt on the floor, peeking in from just outside the door.

"You best stay your distance, young man," Mama Skinner speaks out. Leaning back, Eddie rests his bottom onto his calves, knowing by the tone of her voice that it's for his own good.

Papa Lue comes in from the porch and calls out, "Hazel, how's the little girl doing this morning?"

"It's looking like she's got the fever," Mamma Skinner says back.

"Scarlet?"

"I'd say so. Seems it's got all the making for Scarlet."

In these days, Scarlet Fever could be a serious matter. The rash that came the next morning confirmed it and, with that, all the other children were kept away. The heat still hadn't let up and Papa Lue commented as he headed out the door, "We could sure use a bit of blessings," meaning that the sky needed to open up and rain down on us pretty soon or we were in for some troubling times. Outside, he tended to the chickens and slopped the hogs before the sun came to warm everything.

Mama Skinner decided that it would be best to teach Sunday school herself today; as she didn't think it was right to leave Cindy home, sick as she was. So, after breakfast, she arranged the heavy table so the older kids could sit on top and the younger ones could sit on the bench while Eddie and Popie sat at their feet. The lesson began, as always, with an opening prayer and, when Mama Skinner said amen, the children on the benches repeated her.

A voice spoke from down the darkened hall – a meek voice from a sore throat. As best she could, Cindy echoed, "Amen."

This day, the story of David and Goliath would be told. Mama Skinner shared how the young shepherd would face a giant named Goliath that everyone was afraid to fight. But David, who had protected the sheep from bears and lions, said he would fight this giant. Everyone feared for him because the giant was so big, but David said, "God will be on my side," and he faced the giant with only his sling. The Giant, standing tall with his sword and his armor, looked down upon David and laughed as he knew this little shepherd was no match. But David, armed with only a few stones, feared not. Knowing that God was near and on his side, he placed the smoothest of the stones in his sling and he whirled it to the sky. The stone hit the giant above his eyes and Goliath fell to the ground, dead at David's feet.

All the children cheered after the story was told and they listened as Mama Skinner reminded them that they should never lose faith in God, and that He is always there when you need Him. Once again, they heard the small voice down the hallway say, "Amen."

A sudden crack came from outside that caught everyone by surprise and, after it, several more followed. "Lightning!" yelled the little girl down the hall. Cindy, looking out the bedroom window, yelled it again and then, in her tiny, crackling voice, she yelled, "Fire! The forest is on fire!"

Everyone rushed outside to see that the words she spoke were true: the lightning had ignited the dry hillside at the foot of the forest. As the weeds burned, the fire crept toward the forest and the children all looked at each other, afraid that the trees they all loved to climb and play on would soon be burned.

The smoke from the fire was distant and blew its gray dirty breath over the top of the trees as it climbed the slope, headed for the pines and cedars. In no time, the first of many beautiful trees were gone and more were ablaze.

Cindy began to pray as she sat in front of her window, isolated from the others. Soon, all the orphans joined in as they knelt in a circle by the old woman. What else could they do? They had no other power and they were just children, so they did as Mama Skinner, and they prayed for the fire to stop.

It had been at least an hour and the smoke from the forest fire had shifted. Cindy could smell the freshly burnt cedar as it filled the air around the little farmhouse and she could hear the windows in the kitchen being pulled shut. A sense of panic had overtaken all, and they wondered if the little house itself would be harmed.

As the children continued their prayers, Mama Skinner told them all to go outside and look for Papa Lue who would be coming up with the truck. "When he gets here, you all get in the back, and make sure you hold on to the little ones!" she ordered.

Clearly, they would have to evacuate the little farm but first, the livestock would need to be released. When Papa Lue rolled up, the kids ran to the truck and piled into the back. Papa Lue joined Hazel in opening up the pens and making sure Charlie, the horse, and Tony, the little cow, were free to run. This was a sight: chickens running about and a fat mama sow with piglets wandering out of her pen. The goats were on top of the old shed roof, calling out and the fire continued to run toward the farmhouse.

They were all ready to go when Mama Skinner said, "I'll be right back! I have to get Cindy before we burn to the ground!" Running toward the house, it wasn't but a minute before she came out with the seven-year-old in her arms.

Cindy said aloud, "Mama, let me say good bye to my tree." The old woman, a bit winded, set her down just for a moment and Cindy knelt down and said one more prayer.

"Daddy-God,

Please, I know you can hear me. Please don't let our farm burn to the ground! Please, Daddy-God. Please save all the animals and Charlie and Tony and don't let them be harmed."

Thunder racked the sky and the ground rolled with might as she finished her last prayer. Climbing to her feet, she looked out at the forest burning and once more to the sky as that familiar chill ran up her spine. Then, with the help of the old woman, she began toward the truck.

With one more big flash and another loud burst from the sky, they scampered into the cab as the rest of the children huddled into the back. While the truck pulled around to head out, Papa Lue reached and pulled on the wipers and Cindy, seeming to be fully energized and feeling well says,

"My throat doesn't hurt anymore."

Mama Skinner says, "That's good, honey, 'cuz we're about to get a bad storm." Then she stops, looks across the cab to her husband and they smile. The sky has begun to rain and the fire that was once headed for the farmhouse is being rapidly doused. Papa Lue stops the truck and backs it up.

The children that are in the back now pour out and run for the porch. Eddie climbs onto the old tractor tire that hangs from the tree and is soon joined by his sister who climbs right past him and into the dripping canopy where she calls out to her **Daddy-God.**

"Daddy-God,

Thank You, Daddy-God, for saving my forest and making the fire go away. Mama Skinner always says to remember You will be near when we need You and, just like the story in the Bible says, God is on our side. Thank You for being here on our side."

Climbing down from the tree, soaked to her skin, Cindy looks out to see nothing but smoke left from the brush fire. Mama Skinner calls from the porch and Cindy runs up to her.

"Let me see that throat of yours," she says. Cindy, full of energy and without fever, opens wide. "Well praise the Lord! Your throat, it's all better!"

Standing there with a knowing look, Mama Skinner smiles as she too realizes that, if not the power of prayer, what could it be that has spared her little farm from sure destruction? A smile comes over her, and she looks to the old oak tree and says aloud, "Thank you, Daddy-God."

Hell's Kitchen

"It's time," says Mama Skinner as the dust rolls up into a fluff behind the black sedan. The last bend in the thin road is slowly leading the '55 Buick Special toward the small farmhouse. A red ball burns though white clouds that have lingered since word first came. It's as though they have gathered to wish farewell to the two that looked to the sky so often with wonder.

"Cindy, honey, you best be coming down out of the tree now. Your aunt is here." Slowly, and with the greatest reluctance, she finds her way to the top of the rope and shuffles her feet around the knot just below the branch.

With apprehension in the air and fear in their guts, Cindy and Eddie look at each other. What will they find in this place called California? Who are these people that have come to take them away, and what is an aunt?

She looks nothing like mother, Cindy thinks as they are greeted by Papa Lue.

Clutching his stuffed brown dog, Eddie remains on the porch with Popie near by. Anxiety surrounds his every breath, his toes curled beneath him, stuffed into an old pair of brown oxfords. He never had shoes of his own – no need, for he was still just a tot. But Mama Skinner, in all her pride, was not about to let him be seen barefoot. It took forever to get those shoes on him, with worn out soles and scuffed with holes.

A big man with broad shoulders and a large head steps out and shakes Papa Lue's hand, "Hank Whitsett, nice to meet you." The plump woman with the cropped red hair lifts herself out of the passenger seat. With a cigarette dangling from her red painted lips, she introduces herself as Elaine. From the back seat comes a chubby girl, "Roberta, say hello."

The meeting is brief. They have come to claim their niece and nephew. Like a bounty, they gather them up and place them in the back seat, and say good bye.

~.~.~.~

Sucked into the hot vinyl seat, I feel the warmth radiate through the fabric of my green plaid shirt. The collar begins to itch on my neck as I scrunch up my shoulders and draw my arms to my chest. Reaching out, Cindy squeezes my hand. The strange feelings in our chests unite as we look at each other, knowing that we are no longer safe.

I can feel her tears, still hiding beneath the surface, as we reach the bend in the road that leads to the apple orchards. She breaks her stare and gazes past me to the old oak one last time. Her eyes well full of tears that solemnly roll off her cheeks. At the porch they all stand staring up the hill as we roll slowly away.

Onto our knees, we look out the back window, eyes to the sky and the bend in the glass…

Trailing us as we head to the main road, the Blue Raven appears. It's been over a year since he led Cindy to me where I played in the drainage pipe.

Stopping before we turn onto the main road, we watch the Blue Raven as it circles, then floats to a dive and rests on the old hollow.

Good Bye.

Part II

Toward the kitchen I went, only to be blocked at the doorway by my cousin Roberta. She could hold me back physically, but she couldn't block my eyes from what I would see.

The End of Enchantment

I remember sitting in the back of the '55 Buick sedan. She was black like a stallion with fire engine red interior and a white fin painted into the quarter panel as if she had wings to fly. The car had chrome bumpers and trim along with white walls, all shiny and polished. Thinking back, this car was a classic.

I was almost three. Funny how I can remember certain things so clearly, like it was just yesterday. I sat in the backseat next to Cindy and my cousin Roberta. Cindy was in the middle and I was on her left, holding my only possession, a brown stuffed hound dog with floppy ears.

Hank, my uncle, was a big man – probably six feet tall and an easy 240 pounds. His shoulders filled the whole seat and his head looked like one of those oblong pumpkins, the kind that grew tall, not round. His hair was jet black and slicked back, Johnny Cash style. I don't remember him saying much, but he had a twitch. His hands were big and tan and they shook constantly, even when wrapped around the steering wheel. He wore a red plaid shirt, short sleeved and made of thin cotton, with a plain, white v-neck T-shirt underneath. His big ears poked out on the sides like a Mr. Potato Head. His facial features were large, as was the scar that ran about three inches down his chin. I always thought it was from the war, but I never really knew.

Across from him sat my aunt Elaine. She was short and fat, weighing about 220 pounds with the reddest hair you could imagine. It was chopped short, kind of butch, but thick and brushed straight up about three inches. She was never without a cigarette and, if it wasn't hanging off her upper lip, it was in her hand being flicked often out the wind wing. There was always a serious look on her face, even when she smiled, and when she did I felt like I had better smile back. I remember being scared, having that not knowing feeling. My shoulders hunched forward, my arms in close, feet crossed.

Elaine would rest her left arm across the top of the seat and shift her weight so her back was toward the door. Her posture clearly stated she was the controller of everything, including Hank.

Shortly after leaving Cedar Town, we crossed the Alabama state line and Hank pulled into a diner on the side of the road. It was a big dirt parking lot with few cars, the kind you pull right up to, typical for a roadhouse diner place in the middle of nowhere.

The clouds that had bid us farewell seemed to stay behind, leaving the sky a clear blue, bright with the sun's rays burning into the humid air. Feeling the woolen collar still stuck to my neck, I walked across the graveled lot, my toes curled tightly inside of the undersized shoes. With each step I winced, but let out not a sound, enduring the pain that offset the unknown fears still within me.

I didn't eat much – guess I had no room in my tummy with all those butterflies. Cindy told them I liked peanut butter sandwiches. For years to come, I would hear that was about all I liked to eat back then.

Finishing lunch, we headed toward the car. Hank opened the door and sat me down on the edge of the door's runner. Taking off my shoes, a surprised look crossed his face and he said aloud, "How in the world did you ever get those on?" The cow-brown hard leathers with the toes worn through now lay at my feet, tossed to the floorboard.

What Hank didn't know was that those shoes weren't really mine. Mama Skinner had only put them on me so I'd look presentable. It was nice to have the shoes off since I'd never really had to wear them before. On the farm we just ran around bare footed, all of us.

The trip was a long ride that took several days, and things would happen along the way that affirmed the unsafe feeling deep inside me.

First of all, I had never been in a car before, least that I could remember. Papa Lou would take us kids for a hayride every now and then. We'd all just climb up into the back of the hay cart and he'd pull it on up the road a bit with his tractor. Other than that, it was quite new to me to be in an automobile.

At night, in the pitch dark, the lights from oncoming cars would creep closer and closer as they were coming toward us and then, ZOOM! they'd pass by in a blur.

Getting used to cars passing in the opposite direction, I'd try and look to see a face or the shadow of whom might be inside. Kneeling into the vinyl seat, my chin resting on top of the door panel, I pressed my face against the cool glass. That was my seat, right behind Hank and next to Cindy. I guess they wanted Cindy and Roberta to sit next to each other so they could get to know one another. Elaine reminded us we were to call them mom and dad and that Roberta was our new sister. Taking one look at them, there was no way anybody was gonna believe that.

One thing was for sure: Mama Skinner used to make us take a bath every night. We all took turns in a big old metal tub that she'd bring into the house. Lucky for me she started with the little ones first.

Roberta sure didn't look like she seen a metal tub very often. Even her teeth were a cruddy yellow color with stuff jammed in them, and they weren't too straight either. Mama Skinner always made sure we were real clean before sitting us down and reading the Bible to us; a different story every night.

A few years would go by before I figured out why Hank and Elaine came all the way to Cedar Town for us. As it turned out, they had a little baby boy just about my age. Elaine, constantly on a diet, had left her purse lying on the floor and Robert, her son, got into her diet pills. He didn't survive. Shortly thereafter, they heard that Elaine's sister had left her children at a working farm in Georgia and never came back.

Looked like I was the perfect replacement for Robert. Unfortunately, Cindy was baggage that came along with the deal. That became apparent real quick.

It was early the next morning after having driven through the whole night. Hank had stopped only once for a potty break at a truck stop in the wee hours of the morning. The glare of the sun was bearing through the windshield and, even with visors down, the sun still hindered his vision.

He began to sweat and the droplets rolled down his cheek as well as his neck that had turned deep red in color. The hands that had twitched the day before seemed to almost jump about as he continually adjusted his grip on the steering wheel.

In less than a moment, the lives of my sister and I would be impacted by an action we had never known before and the clarify of the jittery apprehensions that had been with us since the minute we left Georgia would be upon us.

Cindy said out loud, "Why is that man shaking?" referring to Hank and his uncontrollable nervous twitch.

Without hesitation, Elaine rose right on up out of the front seat and took that big old arm of hers off the back rest, giving Cindy a backhand right in the face. That was just a taste of what was to come. With her nose bleeding and tears falling, we stared into each other's eyes, grasping our hands together and holding tight, stunned and scared.

We didn't talk for the rest of the ride less we were asked a question, and then it was yes ma'am or no ma'am. Elaine didn't like that much either. I suppose it made her aware we were terrified of her and were afraid to speak less we were spoken to. That was a long ride, and it seemed to take forever even though Hank drove pretty much straight through, cruising Route 66 right on through the desert.

By the time I settled into the drive, I had a new sense inside telling me this was the beginning of a very different way of life. Through my sisters hand (that I held tight whenever possible) I felt her same energy as she squeezed to reassure me she was close by. Without her touch, I was lost.

The Little Bastard

It was the wee hours of the morning when we hit the state line. Hank decided to continue the drive without resting so, by late morning, we were turning off the interstate and soon there after driving down the shady tree-lined street that led to the middle class neighborhood where our new home sat.

The sun was warm, but I noticed a difference in the way the air felt. It was lighter and cooler than Georgia and the sky seemed brighter too. Fluffy white clouds floated about the blue sky and a breeze filtered the suns rays as they warmed my tanned skin.

Neighbors were pouring out their homes and onto their porches and lawns to see Cindy and I as we emerged from the *black stallion*. Hank had backed into the driveway to make it easier to unload and, as he opened the big black door, I was the first to climb out.

Seeing all the faces looking for the two orphans from Georgia, I gained the first bit of warmth and welcome in their smiles and eyes. Each of them stood with a big smile as we were hustled into the house.

I wasn't used to seeing houses so close together. Fact is, I don't remember ever seeing a house besides the one Mama Skinner lived in. And, of course, back in Georgia there weren't any other houses around, just a big old barn and chicken coupe, pig pen, that kind of stuff. My mind went back to the little farm and the time I fell into the pig pen giving everyone a scare. They all came running before the pigs got to me. I was just climbing along the top rail like I wasn't supposed to be doing and oops! "SPLAT!" Smelly ol' pigs anyhow.

Anyhow, back to Hank and Elaine. This was what you would call a "working class neighborhood." It was a far cry from the farmland of Georgia but, nevertheless, the people were good hearted and, even though the moment was brief, I felt their compassion.

Hank thought they had a big yard but, to us, it wasn't much larger then the pea patch that ran along the side of the barn at Mama Skinner's. Course, we best not tell them that less we get a whooping.

The house had a steeply pitched roof with two long gables and a third that connected the two in the center. The walkway was made of cement and a big concrete porch with steps and the house had lots of big windows. A long driveway you could barely squeeze a car down led back to a building they called *the garage*.

Hank was what you'd call a tinkerer. His garage was full of stuff half broken and hanging off the walls, lots of big ol' rats too. The doors on the garage were more like barn doors that swung open in four different sections with giant, Z-shaped trim and the garage itself actually looked like a small barn. Instead of hay and horses, though, it smelled like oil and grease. Off the back was the work shop he called a shed and inside a big bench piled high with clutter. A large hand-crank-grinder with a wooden spindle-shaped handle on the right side was bolted to the heavy plank top of the bench. The floor was dirt with pea gravel spread real thin and oil stains all about. Lots of stuff to get into, that's for sure, and Hank told me I couldn't go in there unless he was with me.

This shed had a certain feeling about it that consumed me as I crossed through the doorway opening…almost as though it was haunted. A specific odor lingered in the air like that of a rodent's pee. It was eerie and wicked and I could feel a presence of sorts as Hank walked me about.

In the backyard there were three avocado trees and an apricot with broad limbs that hung heavy and low. On the ground underneath them were the remains of dried up and rotten fruit that had dropped months before. The avocado trees were arranged in a triangle about twelve feet apart forming a canopy of shade. Underneath was just dirt with the leaves raked around the trunks. They were big trees with big limbs and I thought to myself, that they would be great for climbing.

The inside of the house was dark with wood trim and wooden floors. The rooms were big with white walls and walnut trim. A narrow kitchen with a breakfast nook was near where the driveway ran down the side of the house. There were three rooms to sleep in connected by long hallways and there was an "outhouse" inside with a real tub you didn't have to fetch water for, a shower, a water toilet, a sink, a mirror and a window. There was another room (through a door from the hallway) that had a funny white machine in it with a hand crank and rolling pins for washing clothes. Mama Skinner would have liked that machine because it took her lots of time to wash clothes in the metal tub with her scrub board.

I had my own sleeping room with a closet and it wasn't long fore Hank built some cabinets with drawers that went from one end of the room to the other. Each drawer had a cut piece of coat hanger that slipped in a small little hole and locked it from opening. I spent lots of time in that room holding my stuffed dog. I had named him Popie after the friend I left behind in Georgia.

Popie and I were inseparable and did everything together. We used to swing in the big tire Papa Lou had hung from a big oak tree with this big rough rope. I used to climb on top of the tire and hold onto the rope while Popie would push and spin me. My hands would get red hot from that rope spinning. If we spun it too much it would start to get knots at the top and then, like a spring, it would spin itself back the other way. Always taking turns, we spent hours playing on that swing.

We used to climb up in the barn in the hay and look out the big opening near the roof or chase the chickens around. I especially liked the chicken coupe because it had this plank with slats about every foot so the chickens wouldn't slip when they walked up it. I used to run up and down it. Now all I had were memories of Popie and, every time I saw my stuffed dog, it reminded me of my friend back in Georgia.

~.~.~.~

Soon after we arrived in California, Elaine became pregnant and, the following April, she gave birth to a baby boy they named Henry. It seemed like Hank and Elaine constantly fought with each other. I sat in my room most of these early days, hearing voices, loud with anger, each out speaking the other. Soon, another sound would follow. Cindy, my sister, was getting yelled at, often getting slapped and punched by Elaine - like that first time in the back of the *black stallion*. Each time this happened I saw my sister change a bit, hardening with a determined look about her face as she was ordered to do all the work while Roberta would sit in front of the television, oblivious to her surroundings.

As for me, I didn't watch much TV. Still very scared, I did my best to stay out of sight. Besides, it was in the front room and I didn't like to go out there because I was afraid I would get in trouble. I used to sit in the hallway, tucked tightly into the crease where the wall and floor came together. It was just outside the dining room that I would peek around the corner of the doorway, just enough to see Hank and Elaine and Roberta watching television while my sister Cindy would be standing on a chair at the sink washing dishes, hands red from the scalding water that filled the sink.

Cindy had to do everything: wash the dishes, clean the whole house, scrub the bathroom, the floors, and the laundry. I fed the dog and emptied the trash in the beginning, and sometimes picked up the oranges that fell on the front yard. It wasn't long before I had my own regimen of chores, although I didn't mind because it kept me connected with my sister and our role in their home.

Soon, I was big enough to help Cindy scrub the bathroom. I did the floor and the shower stall up to the handles as Cindy would do the top half. Once finished, we would summon Elaine to come in and inspect everything. After she would finish her inspection, she would make us go back and scrub the grout lines of the tile again. They never got any cleaner but we did it anyway. Clearly, this was her way of keeping us away from the rest of the family on Sunday evenings as they all watched the television.

This one evening, I remember her taking me by the back of the head, throwing me onto the bathroom floor and yelling at me,

"Scrub it again, and this time do it right!"

As I slid across the floor, on knees that had turned white from the Comet cleanser that had saturated my skin, I came to rest against the corner of the tub near the window of the bathroom.

Standing behind me, she opens the top drawer and throws an old yellow toothbrush at me. It hits me in my shoulder. The door shuts, I hear the little hook fastened into the eye screw from the outside and I know, once again, that I am locked in.

But I am not alone. I can feel my spiritual friend deep within my shoulders and chest, helping to sit me up strong. I find the toothbrush and I sprinkle more Comet in the white lines of the grout. I will be here again for hours.

Then she would slam the door shut and leave me in there for hours while I scrubbed one tile at a time: just me, the rag, a tooth brush, and a green can of Comet, knees white from kneeling in the suds.

I learned to scrub really well but I also learned all about the bathroom and what was in each cabinet and drawer. I knew I wasn't supposed to be opening the doors and drawers but I was curious, especially about the one that was locked.

Elaine would point out all the corners and put my face right up to them and act disgusted because I missed a spot, slapping me in the back of the head for good measure while adding the classic, "you little bastard." Although I was only four years old, I felt a life's worth of weight in my heavy mind. I thought I was being punished but actually it was just the normal way Elaine treated us. She classified me as a "little bastard" because I was born by parents who weren't married. My sister always stood up for me. It didn't matter that she would get beaten – it was all she could do to divert Elaine's aggression away from me.

~.~.~.~

Hank was a truck driver and he went on long hauls running up and down the "Grapevine" (A stretch of road on I-5). He had a good heart but didn't run the house. He knew what was happening and was caught in the middle, his loyalty with Elaine but his heart felt for us, in the beginning that is.

On occasion, he would take me with him when he was making a run to Bakersfield or somewhere close. I had to sneak into the truck without his boss knowing. One time, another driver saw me standing in the yard behind the rig, waiting for Hank to come around and pick me up. I was afraid Hank would get in trouble until the man smiled at me and gave me a wink. I told

Hank about him and he said, "Oh that's just Al. He's okay. He's a good guy." I guess he *was* a good guy because Hank didn't get into any trouble over it.

Hank only took me with him a few times. I remember once, when he took me up into a mountainous area at night. As we drove around the corners I would ask him if he could stop because I saw flashlights lying by the side of the road and I wanted one. He just laughed and said, "Those are 'dead men.'"

I asked what he meant by "dead men" and he said that's what you call an empty can of beer.

My animated mind, though, still sought the desire to stop and retrieve what I believed to be valuable flashlights illuminated by the headlights of the big rig as it navigated the curves that wound about the steep mountainous road up the grapevine. Secretly, I was afraid to admit that my true fear was the darkness at night when I was alone in my room. I saw these beer cans as an answer to my loneliness; vessels of safety to keep me company under the covers, comforting me from the nightmares of the day.

When I wasn't with him on his trips, I looked forward to him coming home because the beatings were less frequent when he was around. Elaine had this brown strap, about two inches wide, that was folded in half. It had a snap but no buckle. She would flail on us with that thing, grabbing us by the shoulder or ear or hair and bringing that strap up over her head, coming down on our backsides ten or twelve times. All the while, she would hold a cigarette between her lips and mumble something like, "Don't you ever look at me like that again, you little bastard!"

It really got to her when I learned not to cry. She would stop, look at me and whip me some more, but it was my way of rebelling. I learned it fast and it had a way of slowing things down a bit.

Cindy wasn't as lucky as me. She would scream and Elaine would get real satisfaction, beating about her backside. Taking both hands and grabbing her by the hair, Elaine would sling her across the room into a wall or any furniture within the path. Sometimes, Roberta would hold me back by blocking the door so I couldn't get in the room.

From my room I heard it coming, a rumble down the hallway. Storming in from the bedroom on their way to the kitchen, the heaviness of their size shook the house. Seconds later, my sister would be screaming and I would run to her.

Toward the kitchen I went only to be blocked at the doorway by my cousin, Roberta. She would hold me back but she couldn't keep my eyes from what I would see: my sister being held with her arms over her head by Hank, from behind, she was completely exposed, with no way to cover up or protect herself…She couldn't get away.

Elaine flailed away, beating her in the face with her fists, over and over as the blood flowed from her nose. Cindy's screams were sickening to my heart and there was nothing I could do.

And then, we would run…

It wouldn't be the only time we would run. Toward the front porch like two little mice escaping the swipes of an alley cat, we would slip away, avoiding Elaine's fury as we found the door and ran from the house. Each time we made it farther and farther away, but the results were always the same. The neighbors must have called because, within a block or two, there would be a cruiser from the police department. The officer would corral us into his car and drive us back, all the time reminding us that if we only kept our mouths shut we wouldn't get in trouble. Little did he know we were literally running for our lives.

Back to the house he would drive us, not knowing really why or what we were running from. The mentality at the time was that children were to be seen, not heard, and child abuse had not yet been identified as a form of domestic violence. We were horrified as we were again delivered into the grasp of these people that beat us with their fists in an ignorant fury.

Hank, too, had a temper. He was a nervous guy with a short fuse.

Most of the time, he would be supportive but his belt came off when he would get mad and, four or five whacks later, we felt welts on our butts and backsides. What really stood out was that neither one of them ever hit Roberta.

One night I went to bed without taking out the trash. I was awakened by Hank pulling me out of the bed and shoving me down the hall onto the back porch. Then when I had the trash in my arms, he placed his hand on the back of my head and shoved me through the screen door. I fell down the two steps onto the driveway and the trash spilled everywhere. He yelled at me for spilling it and I stayed out there until I had finished picking it all up. When I tried to come in I found that the lock on the screen door had been set, so I just sat on the steps and waited for him to come let me in. It was very cold. I felt like a cat waiting at the door for someone to notice and I didn't dare knock.

I hated that particular door. After little Henry was toddling around Hank built a tall fence – about eight foot high – that blocked off the driveway from the front part of the house and another fence that blocked off the drive-way from the back yard effectively turning this area into a long cell block with nowhere to go. When Elaine would get sick of looking at me she would make me go outside and play in that section. I hated being there because it was hot, with nothing but cement to walk around on and I wasn't there cause I wanted to play; I was there so she wouldn't have to look at me.

The morning sun would heat up the side of the house and radiate back on that area making it very uncomfortable. I would stay in the shadowy place next to the neighbors' fence, out of the heat and direct sunlight, trying to stay cool.

Sometimes she'd tell me to sweep the driveway and, when I went out, she would lock the door so I couldn't come in when I finished. I learned how to use a broom real good this way. I also figured out how gravity worked. I would start up by the garage doors and sweep downhill, the whole driveway until I got to the gate. Struggling to open it, I would then go out front and sweep the rest of the drive out into the street. That would be the only time I would get to look out front, so I took my time on that section. It was shady and I could be cool there.

On trash day I took the cans out. They were metal and hard to drag, but I managed. I didn't mind doing chores. We did chores in Georgia, but it was different because everybody pitched in and did their share. Didn't matter who finished first because they would just help you 'til everybody was finished. It didn't seem right that Roberta didn't have any chores to do and Elaine just sat on the couch, smoking one cigarette after another, drinking her coffee. She put her feet up on the coffee table and the bottoms would be black with dirt and her toe nails would be curled over. She would pick her teeth with a match book and leave it in her ashtray. I used to hate cleaning her ashtrays. They were disgusting, with boogers and toe nails in them. You never knew what you would find.

On Sunday evenings we would eat dinner in the breakfast nook. Elaine had a booth built in the corner where we kids sat. Cindy sat at the end closest to the kitchen because she had to get up if Elaine wanted anything – like butter or milk – from the fridge or a plate from the cupboard.

This seemed regimental for Cindy, as if she was a servant. "Cindy, where's the butter? Why isn't there a butter knife on the table? You know I don't like plastic glasses, why did you give me one? Get up and get me a glass one."

Cindy had to be careful because she was right next to Elaine; a mere backhand away. There were many times Elaine would smack the hell out of Cindy for "the wrong look" or not getting up in time. If Elaine told her to get something and she didn't move right away, Elaine would start slapping her in the face and all Cindy could do was try to cover up. This was a normal part of dinner for us and it was all we could do to sit there and try to eat while paralyzed with the fear of being beaten.

One Sunday evening I made the terrible mistake of asking a particular question during dinner. Must have been about five or so in the afternoon, because the sun was still out.

I had heard the name Robert come up in the past, several times.

I didn't know who Robert was and I was curious. Although I was not much for speaking without being spoken to, I braved the moment and asked, "Who was Robert?"

Big mistake.

Hank stood up and reached across the table, slapping me so hard my ears rang and I bounced off the seat of the booth. He then smacked me again, pushing the table as he reached. As he figured he could not get a good swing at me he grabbed my feet from under the table and pulled me with full force, dragging me out from the underside.

Once out, he proceeded…

My back scrapes across the stainless base of the table as he grips my ankle and yanks me to him and I am flung across the kitchen. I roll over, trying to get up and he kicks me in my butt so hard that my body flies off the ground and my head hits the door to the service porch.

The barrage of punches and kicks continue as I am headed back toward the table. Hank grabs me and slams my head into the oven door. I am dizzy with fear and I cannot stand. He picks me up, exhausted, dragging me back to the breakfast nook and shoving me below the table, ordering me to get back into my seat as I try to crawl out of his reach.

I had been beaten many times but, this time, he had a fury in his eyes. I had done something wrong. I had mentioned the name of the son who had died before we were brought from Georgia. This was sacred and the questioning of this subject was something that I should have known better than to bring up. I was informed of this after the beating, of course.

As Cindy, Roberta, and little Henry all watched in horror, Hank threw me back under the table and ordered me to get back into my seat. Eventually, Elaine joined in and said, "You knew better to bring up his name. Don't you ever say his name again, you little bastard!"

During the rest of dinner, not a word was mumbled from anyone. I sat stunned, a knot on the side of my head from the laundry room door, my ribs aching and my ears ringing.

I could feel Hank's breathing as he recovered, huffing and puffing, eyes bulging with anger as sweat poured from his brow. His elbows rested on the table top and his fist was pressed into his left hand just inches below his chin. His glare continued to burn toward me.

Wheezing, I struggled to catch my fleeting breath, my left rib throbbing. My eyes slowly broke from his, lowering to the red Formica table top toward my plate and the green peas upon it.

Running through my four year old mind were only a blur of confused notions. Seldom had I ever spoken my thoughts aloud, and my question was asked only to understand a name that had passed my ears. Yet, to me, this would be significant in defining the difference between speaking only when spoken to and braving the unset boundaries of a family unit.

From that day forward I stopped asking questions of any sort. "Yes," "No," or "I don't know," became standard in my response when I was spoken to. I went to my sister if I wanted to know something and only if she was by herself, so as not to risk the chance that Roberta would hear, for that would surely bring grief to my sister.

~.~.~.~

It wasn't but a few weeks after that night in the kitchen, that Cindy and Roberta began school. This was a very lonely time for me, especially in the mornings. I could hear them leave as they shuffled about getting their lunches ready. Soon I would be up, exploring for hours, waiting for Elaine to wake up. Bored and afraid to turn on the TV, I would sit and hold my stuffed Popie dog, just waiting for Elaine so I could eat.

Eventually, I found how to open the front door, creeping quietly. Wandering out to the steps, I sometimes played with the little yellow moths that landed on the bushes, trying to catch them as they would fly about. It was during one such morning that the lady next door called to me.

"Eddie, honey, are you hungry?" she would say. "Come here, sweetheart. Let me get you something to eat."

Nellie was her name and she would take me inside and set me at her table and make me a grilled cheese sandwich. I think she was the first of my many "Angels," and it became routine for me to slip out of the house as Elaine would sleep in. Like a stray dog, I would stand next to the corner of the house hoping she would see me. In no time, a few minutes at most, she would open the front door and signal for me to come in to eat.

When finished with my sandwich and glass of milk, she would give me a hug and send me on my way. I came to know that look in her eye; that she knew my pain and my loneliness. She also knew how to send me love, even when she couldn't see me. I could *feel* her energy.

She gave me hope. She also gave me a connection to another realm, a place away from here that seemed to help me make sense of the moments that seemed so timeless. She was an internal lift inside of my narrow chest; a similar feeling remembered from the days we were orphans on the farm in Georgia. It was wholesome and calming, Nellie was special like Mama Skinner.

~.~.~.~

One morning, as Elaine slept, I was exploring in the bathroom when I came across Hank's razor. I had seen it before and was curious about the way it opened up and the sharp razor blades inside. At the base of its silver handle was a dial that turned to open the top. This intrigued me, as did the whole grown up idea of shaving. Sometimes I would peek around the corner while Hank shaved and watch him use it. This morning I decided it was time that I learned how so, taking his mug and brush, I placed it in the soap and made a nice lather.

The sensation from the old bristle brush was cold as I put it to my face and dragged it about, mimicking the movements I remembered from spying on Hank. It dried quickly and left my face feeling sticky and tight.

Ouch! I cut myself, not just once but several times. Still, I was determined to keep going and nicked my face severely. When I finished, I put away everything so Elaine wouldn't find it. Then, with blood dripping from my face, I went back to my room and crawled under the sheets, scared, for I knew I would be in big trouble. The superficial cuts were staining the white sheets with little red dots about the size of a quarter as I hid underneath them.

After a while I heard Elaine getting up. She was a heavy woman and made plenty of noise when she walked down the hall. She must have come across the blood on the floor and started following it. I could tell by the noise of her walk where she went: first, back to the bathroom then into my room where it was off with the covers.

She must have thought I tried to kill myself because she was shocked and confused until I showed her the razor in the cabinet. After that, Hank put locks on all the cabinet doors in the bathroom. He was out of town when this happened and I remember him talking to me but not being angry. Elaine wasn't really angry either, but she did seem kind of bothered about the whole thing.

Perhaps this was more a matter of neglecting a small child prone to exploring: an act of sharing in the responsibility of what happened.

After little Henry got a bit older, Elaine started working. She left early in the mornings to work at Granny Goose Potato Chips. When she returned, she would bring home boxes of the reject chips. It seemed like chips were our main staple those days. I can remember eating bag after bag without stopping.

When Elaine would leave, she left Roberta in charge. Roberta would tell me to get her this or that, generally bossing us around. Fetching stuff for Elaine was one thing but we weren't as cooperative with Roberta, after all, she and Cindy were the same age. I learned to ignore her as I knew there was no way Cindy would let her do anything to me.

Even though I learned not to fear her, the times she locked me in the closet stayed with me, not letting me out even to go to the bathroom. Yes, I urinated in the corner like a caged animal with no way to escape, only to be punished by Elaine when she discovered the odor.

Generally, my life seemed quite boring. I did not have many things to do that I enjoyed. I liked to climb the trees and explore my surroundings but, mostly, I found myself seeking solitude.

The occasional sight of a neighbor kid from behind the closed windows – or even an adult – reminded me that sanity was just beyond that door. The only problem was getting to the other side.

Although I was quite young, I picked up on the not-so-subtle-difference in the way they were treated. Cindy was always busy with chores as Roberta called out for a soda or ordered me to clean my room. She was just like her mother in so many ways, including her contempt for my sister. Of course, I was too young not to blame her but, really, how could you find fault? After all, she was groomed that way by her mother and father; to be in control; to be lazy and to expect others to do things for her. There was no accountability other than to tell on us when her mother returned. Depending on the day, Elaine might scold or punish us or, sometimes, just ask for her coffee.

These pre-school days were filled with defining incidents of great contrast to our days in Georgia. Adapting to the regimen of chores was one thing, but the physical abuse and lack of love left me leery and insecure. The episodes of fleeing for our lives with a bleeding nose or a fat lip – only to be returned by the police who were supposed to protect us – added to the instability of the environment inside that house.

The automatic flinch that a child makes when a hand is raised can be learned only one way: through the experience of its impact upside your head. This was well known by the both of us and a safe distance was kept whenever possible just in case we were to be in the vicinity when our aunt or uncle lost their temper.

I learned solitude from circumstance, like being locked out of the house all those times to sit in the hot sun; or finding all the different colors in a flowering bird of paradise plant as I waited for the door to be opened. I still remember the chalky smell of plaster as I sat on the side steps on a rainy day with my nose just inches away, hoping my aunt would return to unlock the screen's latch and let me in.

We were two orphans from a land far away that came from Georgia knowing a life of fairness and full of care. An evening prayer to end the long days and a safe place to lay our heads is what we knew as a life past.

Our innocence had been lost, left somewhere between Cedartown and the California state line. With it I saw my sister's spirit dissipate. Not long thereafter, perhaps that evening at the dinner table, sitting with the wind knocked out of me, mine followed.

Marking a Thief

Although Fremont Elementary School was just around the corner from our house, the neighborhood dynamics did not favor white kids. We went to Wilson Elementary a few miles to the east instead. I had the morning session and Cindy and Roberta would walk me there, but I would walk home by myself. I enjoyed school but was shy and I didn't make a lot of friends. I found it more comfortable to be standoffish.

Most of the kids who attended Wilson were white. Our neighborhood had a cultural mix and Elaine and Henry weren't about to let us go to school with "a bunch of Mexicans." They had a clear dislike for Mexican Americans, to the point that I remember Hank once saying, "I would rather see you marry a nigger than a Mexican." Even as a child, I understood by their tone how vile this was to say.

I was a quiet student and played by myself, usually on the swing or in the sandbox where I kept my eyes out for some kid's milk money that may have been dropped. Introverted, I spent most of the time just watching the other kids interact; observing but seldom engaging.

The teachers would walk us in two lines, one boy and one girl, to the restrooms where we would wait for our turn. It didn't matter if we needed to or not, we still went. This one boy, I remember, who – even though he was bigger than most of us – had a big insecurity. When he would go into the restroom he would pull his pants down to his ankles and stand at the urinal. The other boys would poke fun at him and point to his bottom and laugh while he stood there. Soon, he would be crying and, in his frustration, start yelling at them to leave him alone.

When this happened, I felt bad for him. This was one of my first experiences of cruelty toward someone other than my sister or me and, inside, I felt his hurt. It was just sad to see him so frustrated and crying, pleading to be left alone.

One day, early in spring, I was walking home from school down Washington Street. It was a fair afternoon with some overcast creeping in. I had switched to the late session in kindergarten and was about halfway home when I came across some change on the sidewalk in front of a house. It was nothing much: a quarter and a few dimes, maybe a nickel or two.

How exciting it was to find all this money! Even though I was well past the market I turned around and went right back to spend what I had found. It was an anxious minute or two as I ran all the way back toward Bristol Street to the little market next to the butcher shop.

I hadn't been in there too many times before but I knew what I wanted and it was right there behind the clerk. I spilt my change out on the counter and pointed at various boxes of candy bars, bubble gum and other sweets until all of my money was gone. The clerk was a tall man with light hair and a nice smile. He was very helpful, explaining what I could buy with the last few cents, then he put all the candy in a small brown bag and I went on my way.

Walking home to my aunt's house, I took my time and enjoyed the candy I had purchased. Normally, it would have taken about twelve minutes for me to get home from the point where the market was but this day I'm sure it took longer. I wasn't in a hurry and I was eating one treat after another.

When I finally did get home I found myself in major trouble, not realizing how it must have looked to my aunt: a kid with all that candy and no resources with which to purchase it. She immediately concluded that I had stolen it. She asked where I had gotten the candy and, when I tried to explain, she started slapping me around and calling me a liar and a thief. I tried to convince her that I truly *did* find the money as I said but she continued to beat me anyway.

What she did next was astounding and truly became a defining moment of my childhood. She dragged me by the hair and threw me into the car. Then she drove me to the market, all the while holding a cigarette in her mouth. I can remember the exact route she went and how scared I was. When she pulled into the parking lot, I felt a sense of relief because I knew I had done nothing wrong and she would soon find out that I had been honest with her.

Taking a hold of me just under the shoulder, her fingers dug into my armpit as she lifted and pulled me along. She marched me into the store demanding to speak to the manager and drawing the attention of everyone. Then, still in her grasp, she shoved me forward. Presenting me to an audience of customers she proceeded to inform the clerk that he had been victimized by "this little thief."

The clerk was amazed and immediately interrupted saying that this little boy had paid for the candy. Elaine insisted back, assuring him that I was a thief and that he need not defend me, she knew better. She went on to inform him that my father was a thief, so surely, I was a thief. Intent on making her point, she went as far as to suggest to him that, while his back was turned, I reached behind him and took the candy from behind the counter.

The clerk was adamant about remembering me and went on to explain to Elaine why he kept the candy behind the counter as well as to give her a complete inventory of the items purchased and the exact amount of money I had spent. He pointed out to her the obvious, as he referenced the bag that held the remaining candy, "Perhaps he stol' the bag also."

They were actually arguing and this man was defending me. I can't begin to explain the feeling I had. To know that someone was standing up for me and telling Elaine I was not the terrible little person she made me out to be nearly brought tears to my eyes.

The argument subsided, both sides maintaining their position as Elaine grabbed hold of my arm again and stormed out. She opened the car door and threw me in, proceeding to drive down Washington Street, not the *least* convinced that I had been telling the truth. As she drove past the house that I had found the money in front of I was afraid she was going to stop and tell them, but she didn't. She kept driving, even though I pointed out where I had found the money.

When we arrived back at the house, Elaine stormed out of the car and caught me in just a few steps. I was headed for the house and I knew what was coming, but I didn't know everything. She dragged me into the house and slapped me across the back of the head several times and then threw me into the bathroom and told me not to move. As I stood in the bathroom scared and not knowing, she returned with a metal pan and informed me,

"In Old England, when somebody was caught stealing, they would be marked so all would know they were a thief. That way, they would be publicly recognized."

As I stood at the sink with my hands over the basin, she poured the liquid from the pan she had returned with. Slowly, I felt the warm green liquid drenching my hands and forearms.

She orders me to turn my palms over and continues to pour the liquid substance over the other side of my hands and forearms. My fingernails are staining like the rest of my skin and I cry out inside to my inner soul, asking why she's doing this.

I feel a rush within my chest. My spiritual visitor has once again returned to hold me strong.

Elaine had poured food coloring over my hands and up my wrists about three inches. She said that now everyone would know I was a thief and would know to beware of me.

I was devastated. No longer scared of Elaine, I was scared that everyone who saw me would think I was a thief and that I was a bad person. Starting that day I washed my hands for several minutes at a time. I used Lava soap that my uncle had kept in the bathroom to clean the grease off his hands after working on cars – fifteen or sometimes twenty times. All day long I would wash my hands, sometimes even using Comet, remembering how it turned my knees white, just hoping to fade the green a little more with each wash. It was useless.

The kids at school wanted to know why my hands were green but I gave no explanation. I was shy, so it wasn't a big deal that I didn't answer. Day after day went by as the green slowly faded.

Then, after about ten days, my aunt told me to go into the bathroom again. Once there, she began scolding me, not *yelling* but methodically explaining to me that I was wrong trying to wash my hands so much; that I was trying to be sneaky and that my punishment was not complete. She then colored my hands green again and told me I was not to try and wash them clean. This time it took several weeks for the green to fade. I again faced ridicule and kids thought I was weird.

Strange, not one person ever asked if I was a thief. I was confused. Elaine had painted my hands green to show the world that I was a thief. The world didn't seem to associate green hands with anything; it only provoked puzzled looks from adults and teachers.

Hank and Elaine seemed to have a distinct view of how children played a role in society. Elaine used to say "Do as I say, not as I do," "Speak only when spoken to," "Children are to be seen, not heard," or, "When I was a child I got *one* pair of shoes that had to last me till I outgrew them."

This always hits home when I think about the day I was walking from school and the streets were getting new blacktop. They were cement with large cracks in them and the cracks had been filled with black rubber. This particular day, workmen had coated the entire street, end to end, with this rubberized asphalt. There was absolutely no way across, so I thought I would run as quickly as I could, and I did. By the time I crossed three streets full of this stuff I had filled the entire treads of my tennis shoes and had about a quarter inch of black stuff caked onto the bottoms.

I was in big trouble when I got home and, of course, there was no use explaining. Elaine gave me the belt and sent me outside were I left my shoes and told me to clean them. I was out there for hours rubbing them on the grass and dirt trying to break free the fresh asphalt. That afternoon, Hank came home and gave me his pocket knife so I could scrape off what I could. He gave me some paint thinner and a rag and I cleaned them some more. They never came clean but at least I was able to get the mass of asphalt off.

I was glad when I finally was rid of those shoes because they felt awkward wearing them with the little lumps on the bottoms.

It's amazing how things happened in my life. After about a month those shoes would prematurely be destroyed while trying to mow the lawn. Looking back, I was a bit young to be mowing the yard with a power lawn mower. It took every bit of muscle I had just to pull the rope.

On this sunny weekend morning, while pulling the rope, I slipped. My right foot went under the edge of the mower as it started. I froze stiff as I felt the whirl of the blade breeze above my toes. Slowly reaching, I was able to pull the wire off the spark plug and kill the engine. Once the blade had slowed, I pulled my foot out from under the mower. My heart continued to race as my eyes deceived me. The top of my tennis shoe was sliced away from the rest of the shoe. As I walked into the house, it flapped with each step. The look on Elaine's face was that of amazement as she told me to be more careful next time. A few days later, I got a new pair of sneakers.

Sometimes I wondered if Elaine had a clue as to her impact on us. I wouldn't make a move without permission because I didn't want to get in trouble. One day, I was really hungry so I asked her while she was in the kitchen if I could have a banana. She seemed shocked that I would ask and told me I didn't have to ask for something to eat, I could just help myself. I got a chair and went over and got a banana from atop the refrigerator. I really thought that was nice of her. I knew I could make myself a peanut butter sandwich and a glass of milk without asking but I never dared get anything other than that.

~.~.~.~

That summer, I spent time with Hank's parents in south Santa Ana. They lived in a poorer section of town known as Cross Warner. This was one of the older parts of Santa Ana, and they had moved there back in the 1930's.

Hank's dad was really tall and he spent lots of time in his garage. His garage looked a lot like the barn back in Georgia. It was big, about thirty feet wide, and had room for three cars. I called him grandpa and watched him work on his cars as I sat nearby. He had built their house during the war period when materials were scarce.

They had a big avocado tree filled with huge fruit that covered most of the roof. I would pick them and Cindy, Roberta, and I – and sometimes little Henry, too – would pull around a wagon and sell them for money to go to the theater on Sundays.

Hank's mom was always busy feeding the birds in her aviary or tidying up around the house and yard and I knew her as grandma. Their house was spotless. Even though Roberta and little Henry were their real grandchildren, they always treated Cindy and me very special, especially me.

Whenever Hank would visit and bring me along, they would ask if I could stay for the night and the extra bedroom was fixed up for me. I felt so loved by them. They were always so patient and showed me everything. Their whole house was in order and made such sense to me. Sometimes, when grandpa would mow the yard, I would go out and rake the leaves with him. They didn't make me but I wanted to help. It reminded me of Georgia where everybody chipped in.

Grandpa's garage had a dirt floor and lots of oil had been poured on it to keep the dust down. Compared to my uncle's garage, the walls had a lot less stuff on them and none of it was broken. Grandpa's cars were polished like mirrors and even the wheels where shiny. They had a lot of pride and dignity in their lives and I loved being with them. Whenever Elaine would get furious with me, I would hope she would send me there. Sometimes she would and, except for Cindy, I wished I would never have to go back.

Defining the Ignoramus

As time went on, the beatings intensified and varied from the belt to punches and kicks.   Cindy always got it the worst and, many times, the beatings drew blood. When we knew we were going to get it, we hoped for the belt because we knew what to expect, even though it was terrifying the way Hank would pull it off. Usually in a fit of rage, he would hit us as hard as he could. Being a big man, just coming at us was enough to scare us half to death. But, when he got a hold of you, he inflected real pain with real intent. He didn't care where the belt hit and, when he was done, we would have welts on our legs for days. The good thing about Hank and his belt was that he couldn't take more than a few steps without his pants falling off. He would have to stop and pull them up three or four times during the beating. By the time he was finished sweat would be pouring off his forehead.

Usually we got the belt but, lots of times, it was the backhand or an open-handed-slap upside the head. With Hank, it was spontaneous and usually the result of some unreasonable agitation. For example, on the weekends Hank would do his back yard mechanic stuff and I always helped. Not as a matter of choice: this was required. Fortunately for me, I liked helping because I learned about cars and what made them work. Mainly, I was in charge of fetching the wrenches and various tools like jack stands and such.

The jack stands were home-made out of an old truck axle. He took apart a differential that bolted together and then sliced off the axle housing about eighteen inches up and cut a concave shape into it so it could accommodate a car's axle and support it solidly. Compared to the shaky bumper jacks, they provided greater stability and peace of mind when we worked under the car. The only drawback was they weighed a ton and I couldn't carry them but one at a time. This seemed to bother Hank because he could just stack them and carry them both with one hand.

If he sent me after a half inch open end and I couldn't find it I knew I was going to get yelled at. He'd send me back and if he had to go get it himself, I was for sure going to get smacked in the back of the head. If I didn't move quick enough, he would kick me in the butt to hurry me along. It got to the point where I was afraid to go look for something because I might not find it and then I would be in trouble.

He would call me an "ignoramus" when I couldn't find something or he was mad and this was often. One of the worst things would be when he would send me to the garage for a tool then he would yell, "Eddie!" I would have to run back because he forgot something. I didn't mind the running back and forth part, it was the yelling of my name that sent chills up my spine. The whole neighborhood would hear and it would embarrass me and make me feel like he thought I was stupid. If I did bring back the wrong tool he'd say angrily, "God Damn It! I said the Phillips not a regular.

I found myself starving for affection and striving for approval. I began to understand that I could not win, nor could I please him, even though he would surprise me sometimes and tell me at the end of the day what a big help I was. This was to me like rubbing the tummy of a puppy. He wouldn't know it but, when I was by myself, I would cry silently, for a moment only, for I didn't want to be discovered by anyone.

Sometimes we would get beat at the same time. It was usually on the weekend and, many times, Elaine used the words "for good measure." This referred to all the things we did wrong that they didn't know about.

Although we knew we didn't deserve it, we would stand in defiance and take it anyway. Cindy, always more emotional, would scream as she received hers. I would not. I sensed Elaine and Hank had a feeling of satisfaction when Cindy would react and this, I believe, fostered the birth of my own style of rebellion.

Elaine was the one really dishing it out. I remember Cindy bleeding from the nose, grabbing my hand and, once again, we were running out the front door. We would run down the street as fast as possible, Cindy crying, as she dragged me along.

At first it was Hank who would come after us. He would catch up to us and set us down, try to reason with us and say he was sorry, then bring us back. However, as time went on, Hank starting dishing out the beatings. Then it would be the police that would come after us and bring us back.

The police had no idea, in those days, what child abuse was. They did not understand mental abuse or how a child's spirit was being damaged. How could they not understand the problems? Sometimes they would be out several times a month. Each time, we would run faster and farther. Cindy was running for her life; I simply hung on and tried not to slow her down.

When the police would bring us back, I could count on the neighbors to be out front. It was as if they all knew what was happening and they were standing there in silent support for us when we would be returned. I just wondered why this happened. I think these times, too, were defining moments. As a very young child I could see how things worked. I could also see that things did not work with children in mind but, in spite of that, clarity began to shine.

Too many things were happening. Our actions and behaviors were no different than those of their own children. The sense of right and wrong began to take hold in my mind as I realized at this very young age, that I was not the one who was messed up.

I also found a peripheral support system. At night, I would sit in my room and watch the lady next door as she washed the evening's dishes. With the lights out I could see right into her window, the contrast of two different worlds illuminated for me to observe.

There were peaceful tones in her voice as she directed her children and joyful laughter streamed through the window as they played at the table. While Elaine and Roberta and little Henry sat in the living room watching television, I watched my own show. It was a story about love, compassion and parenting without violence or raised voices that gave me insight far beyond my years.

I knew there was something terribly wrong at the Whitsett's house.

A Rebel is Born

.

Entering the first grade, I had become uniquely introverted, possessing a quiet persona on the outside. However, on the inside, I was far from this. My mind raced to take in all the new adventures exposed to me once outside the confining walls of that house.

Every observation was an assessment of the moment. There was a whole new world filled with excitement and new experiences and, most of all, independence. Albeit limited, I still had, for the first time, the opportunity to reflect on the day's events. Some might call it daydreaming. I would say it was my first true taste of freedom and I was taking it all in.

I've heard it said that you don't know what you're missing if you never had it to begin with. I suppose that would be me. I knew nothing about interaction short of what went on inside the walls at home. I had been isolated from all others the first few years by the panes of glass in windows that were always kept shut. So was my mind; isolated and contained, imprisoned in a compartment without social interactions of any sort.

I found myself in internal conflict, fighting the realization that I was being short-changed the opportunities other children my age enjoyed. I saw their laughter and joyful moments on the blacktop as they intermingled with each other. Their carefree dispositions seemed so natural, yet I didn't dare attempt such silliness. I stood on the sidelines, shy and in the back, with a mind full of questions as I processed my life's balance sheet and assessed my net worth. My value system was truly out of balance.

I learned it was okay to smile when someone said hello and, eventually, I whispered, "hi," in reply. The warmth of others around me slowly rubbed off as I cracked the cocoon that surrounded my social restraints. Slowly, I was finding myself in an interactive orchestration of normalcy.

Internally, I felt like a volcano wanting to erupt. Bitterness brewed an angry disposition when I would re-enter the house after a school day that I wished would never have to end. But it did end and I *did* re-enter what felt like an odyssey of ignorance and disgust. The coffee table filled with debris, an ashtray overflowing with the butts of Newport filters intermingled with toenails and other remnants from my aunt's day in front of the television.

Now sharing a room with my cousin, little Henry, my first task was to pick up his mess, then keep him entertained. Soon, Cindy would be home and the routine of the evening would begin, as would the cat and mouse game of staying out of view.

I was learning how to avoid trouble by staying out of sight and saying very little. I was also learning how to rebel from the world I had known for the last few years. Understanding the double standard it represented was only a part of my frustration. The daily abuse of my sister was another.

"Cindy!" I would hear and my sister would literally run from her room down the hall as she responded,

"Yes?"

"Why haven't you started that pile of ironing I set out?" And then it would begin. The outrageous requests of my aunt, "Take out your retainer so it doesn't get broken." My sister would obey and lay it on the ironing board, standing ready for the series of face slaps as they began and weathering the ridiculous assault to its end.

Despite my new social skills, I now battled a different torment... something new to me. I now understood what anger was and, unresolved, it turned my frustration into a sort of depression that was offset by a need to get even for the out-of-balance wheel that wobbled about my day. I gave up, so to speak, caring about anything but getting out of that house.

On the playground I learned that children deal with conflict and find resolution. One may get mad and show anger, and another might toss a fit. But, eventually, it worked out, even if it took the intervention of the playground monitor; another mechanism to address social fairness and keep things in harmony.

This observation also ignited a fire within me. At my core I had a deep and relentless burn that ate at me. I wanted to be like everyone else, but my circumstances would not allow for this, so I accepted my differences and began to find my own way to balance my spirit. Reduce the wobble so to speak.

I had a craft of my own, developed to counterbalance the indifference exposed by my social interactions. I became the sneak my aunt so often accused me of being and I rebelled in the most amazing fashion. I began revisiting behaviors of the past. As if I was more comfortable limiting my engagement with others, I stayed my distance, isolating myself in the shadowy structure of my own survival mechanisms.

There was no time for homework nor was there guidance offered, so when we were finally assigned take-home work, I engaged a plan to beat the system at both ends. I would have no need for help with my homework because I was special and had devised a master plan that seemed foolproof.

Finding it hard to pay attention, I easily became bored and the desire to try hard in school had evaporated because I had no reason to. Having little hope and no understanding of who I was or where I came from seemed to send the signal that I had no purpose. I had been labeled a thief and had my hands painted green a year before, and now realized the true unfairness of my situation. As a six year old, I couldn't even care less about tomorrow. My spirit had been severely strained, perhaps even broken.

My vision was poor, so I sat toward the front of the class in the first row. Each morning during roll call, the children in my class were busy pulling out their homework and getting it ready to pass forward for collection. My teacher, with her eyes down reading from her list, was clueless of my actions.

As the papers would come forward I would take out my red crayon and wait for the perfect moment when no one was watching. When I felt it was clear, I would take the paper from the girl sitting a few seats back and bring it to the top of the stack. Peeking around, making sure again no one was watching, I scribbled her name out with abstract lines, making it impossible to read. I would then print my name at the top, always in the same spot, using the same red crayon.

I did this without being discovered all through the first grade. I did become the sneak that my aunt said I was and I was getting good at it. I had found a way to keep from doing my work and not be punished for it. More than that, I was, for the first time *in control.*

No one, not my teachers or aunt or even my sister knew what I was doing and it felt great to have this power. I kept this secret for the whole year, never getting discovered, finding strength in the ability to actually do something deceitful and not have to pay for it. I was rebelling from authority and finding a way to do so without getting pounded. Each day when I walked home, I felt a sense of strength and independence fostering my feelings of needing no one. This was my first taste of empowerment: life on my terms, toll free, at least for the moment.

As the school year progressed, I settled into my routine and coped with home life as best I could. Having this little ritual with the red crayon seemed to offset the misfortune of abandonment, neglect and abuse. It was my scale of justice, constantly adjusting to counterbalance and get even. So what if it was a secret that couldn't be shared? Although numb inside, I learned to coast through my ordeal.

As with all of us growing up, I too faced a moment of truth that made me stop and ponder my direction and interpretation of parental actions. One morning, when the recess bell rang, I ran from the building toward the playground, racing for the swings. It was a gloomy day in the winter and the sky was full of heavy clouds filled with rain just waiting to burst. The color of the day had little contrast, mostly gray except for the strip of grass just beyond the ruts under the leather straps that hung from the long steel chains.

Hastily I ran determined to be first aboard rather than first in line for one of the three swings. Outrunning my own feet, I tripped and fell violently. Saving injury to my face, I pushed off the rushing ground with my hands and, in doing so, scraped my palms severely. The cuts were deep and there was actually dirt from the black top embedded into my skin that I could not wash out. I clearly had visual injuries, however, this was not so uncommon for a six year old and no special attention was paid to the wounds as they became infected.

A few days went by and the infection increased, creating a pinkish line up to my armpit where a huge bulb of redness swelled. Still, I did not say anything as I interpreted my injuries incorrectly and was afraid I would be in trouble. As fate intervened, the dynamics of home life exposed my wounds for me and perhaps even saved my life.

Later that evening I was getting yelled at by Elaine. It was after dinner and I had not yet taken out the trash. She was quite mad and grabbed a hold of me by the armpit yanking me up toward her oncoming backhand. Uncharacteristically, I screamed in pain and, when I did, Elaine was startled. She let go, stepped back and with a stern but startled look on her face, asked what was wrong. Again, I said nothing but she noticed my hand and the redness. Taking my shirt off over my head, she gathered me and off we went. The next thing I knew, we were at the hospital and they were treating me for blood poisoning.

The pain was severe during the treatment and, like most six year olds, I was terrified. I lay on the hospital bed and a doctor stood over the top of me with a very bright light. It hurt so much when he touched me and it seemed like hours before the pain stopped.

Sometime during the procedure Hank left us there. He was gone for quite some time and, when he returned, he brought me a toy airplane and delivered it with a hug and warmth in his eyes.

Once the procedure was over, we left the hospital and I remember how special I felt with my new toy. I kept it for years because it symbolized an action I was not used to. He *did* care, even though he did not know how to say it. There was something about him. Deep inside, he had a strand of compassion that occasionally surfaced and it was usually at times when it really counted, like the times he would run after us as we fled when we were younger.

It was actions like these that were hardest to comprehend. Here I was, in the emergency room, and Hank was demanding that I be seen immediately. Elaine, too, insisted urgently to get a doctor to see me yet, just a brief time before, she was rearing her hand back to strike me for not taking out the trash. All the while, Hank sat on the couch, fuming and calling me an ignoramus.

I was confused but, perhaps for the first time ever, I felt affection and concern from them both. I sat in the back seat as we drove home and I held tightly to the toy airliner Hank had given me, admiring the decals and twirling props of the expensive gift.

Sitting there a thought hovered in my mind as I sensed the seriousness of my injuries. I was able to realize their actions were that of compassion and that they actually cared about me. Hank, I believe, was scared more than anything. That's why he came back with the gift.

Still, I couldn't help but fear this moment would be short lived, just like the moments when he ran after us, calling out and sitting down on the edge of the curb, telling us he was sorry and to come back home. Yet I hoped for more. My heart *yearned* for more and I soaked up every little bit. I learned about affection that night and understood how starved I was for it.

Yes it has been said that you can't miss something that you never had but, once you get it, you've got to have more, and a small taste can be worse than none at all. For me, I was thankful for that small taste of affection. It brought me a bit closer to the center of the family unit and reduced the wobble just a bit. As things turned out, this moment wore off, but I learned to seek affection anyway: approval for a job well done or a good deed, perhaps "feeling appreciated" would be a better phrase. Regardless of what one calls it, I learned the value of acknowledgment.

A Lesson In Karma

Summertime was a challenging adjustment because the opportunity to get away from the house seemed non-existent. With little to do and in charge of entertaining Henry, who was now about three and had interests typical for his age, I felt trapped and confined. Furthering my frustration was the expectation and accommodation of him always getting his way.

So, my days went from escaping to a school that was stimulating and social, to life in the backyard. At twice his age, I had little interest in making mud pies in the sand box. Instead, I opted for army men and a war zone with tunnels and fortresses made of sand. Eventually, I settled back and accepted my boundaries as temporary, making the best of them.

Occasionally, the kids next door would poke their heads over the scalloped wall to see what we were doing. Sometimes they would even invite us over to play. Seldom granted the privilege of being allowed to visit or play with them, I would be thrilled if permitted, as it meant escaping my uncomfortable environment for a while.

The energy I felt exiting the door and crossing the little curb that separated our front yards was distinct. Entering their home, the scent of warmed tortillas lifted me as I left behind my unhappiness and found my way toward their backyard. Along the way, I received a welcoming smile from Nellie as she tended to preparing us lunch. I was a couple years older than the girls and the boy, David, was about the same age as Little Henry, giving me temporary reprieve from babysitting. This interaction seemed friendly and comfortable, safe and wholesome.

As the days wore on I pressed my boundaries and wandered out to the front steps, using the excuse that I had to pick up oranges that had fallen from the tree. Eventually, I was allowed to hang out in front on the steps where I could see neighbors in their yards interacting with each other. A friendly wave to me or a received smile had a significant effect in lifting my spirits.

Sometimes I would climb the orange tree and pick the fruit that was a challenge to reach. It was risky, inching out on the thin little limbs trying to dodge the sharp thorns that scratched my arms and legs. Keeping a keen eye out for spiders, I would have to watch closely when reaching past a web. The orange tree represented a different type of solitude. This was a freedom of sorts, an opportunity for me to be in control of my time. Even if it was only about picking oranges, it distracted me and helped me to escape my burdened mind.

Learning to toss them softly, just right so they didn't break on landing, I entertained myself by harvesting the little green baby oranges for another day. These made great projectiles that could be launched from the backyard with an old tennis racket borrowed from the garage wall. I would send them flying in an arc through the sky to land three or four houses down.

My responsibilities, of course, included keeping the oranges off the grass. This I tended to daily. When the Santa Ana winds came hundreds would fall to the ground, creating a mess and keeping me busy until the winds settled. Many times, when Hank came home late at night, he would wake me and make me go out in the dark and pick up oranges in my pajamas. This was punishment for not keeping them off the grass. When I would come back in, I was weary of the smack on the side of the head, or a kick in the butt as I went off to bed.

One night in particular, I remember hearing him come in. It must have been late and he had been drinking. He and Elaine began arguing and, as their voices carried, I awoke. He was angry and drunk and in a foul mood. He yelled for me as he walked into my room and I found myself being grabbed and pulled from the top bunk. He reeked of alcohol and oil from driving his tanker truck. The odor had such a distinct smell that I remember it still to this day.

He began slapping me and shoving me, directing me as I stumbled down the hall. I heard my sister cry out, but she was told to shut up as Elaine began threatening her. Onto the front porch he pushed me and then picked me up and threw me off the steps to the lawn, for what I wondered. Was it the few oranges that had fallen after I went to bed?

No, there was more to this incident than that.

With the oranges in my hands and juice running up my arms, I dared to walk past him into the house. I knew it was coming, just as it had so many times in the past, but tonight would be different.

Being picked up, I am thrown through the swinging door of the kitchen. I land sprawled on the floor with my head pressed into the base cabinet of the sink.

I lift myself up. My head has the sensation that a bump like an egg was coming off it, and juice from the oranges squished into my pajama top. Quickly, I clean the mess off the floor and wait for him to step aside before I try to get to my room. As I pass him, he slaps me from behind with his open hand in my right ear so hard that it rang half way through the next day. The burning prickly heat of the pain lasted for days.

I crawl back into bed, pulling the covers up and sliding as close to the wall as I can, out of his reach.

This was another defining moment as I realized he was a mean and angry man who would take his aggressions out on me to offset his own unhappiness. A bully, I now knew, was not something I could have any control over. I would have to accept that I would be his punching bag if I didn't find a way to deal with this.

This was the first time he had ever taken frustration out on me. I began to figure out that I was not the one that was messed up, the Whitsett's were, and I wondered how much they regretted us being there.

That night things changed, and my mind kicked into a new gear and tenacity began to develop. I realized I would have to stay out in front of them, thinking ahead about everything that could happen before it did and anticipate the beating that would be coming regardless. That night, I learned to shut off my feelings of physical pain as well as my emotional torment. I was at war, but the enemy had all the weapons. I only had myself, my fortitude from within and my desire to survive. I realized my spirit was rising in defiance of his actions and that I must find a way to survive.

~.~.~.~

That same summer, I learned about karma in a round about way. Hank and Elaine took me with them when they went shopping for groceries. It was a Saturday morning and we were all in Hank's '59 pink Cadillac. This is the one with the fins that came up off the back quarter panels.

We went to the old A&M supermarket on 1st Street near Raitt, across from Consumer City. With two shopping carts full of groceries, we took our place in line, waiting to move forward. Hank was always in a hurry, I think it was the little white pills he took to keep him awake when he drove his truck for work. I think this added to Elaine's foul mood. I must not have realized that the line had moved, because *bam!* she hit me right upside my head with a push. Elaine's big paw landed hard, sending me flying into a large display of liquor bottles. The impact from the collision caused the whole stack to come crashing down, breaking several bottles and making a ton of noise. Every eye in the store was on Elaine and while some of the looks were of amazement, others from those close-by were of outrage.

As the clerks attended to the mess, Elaine pulled me up and sent me out to the car to wait for them. I wondered how that was going to work out because everybody saw her slap me and saw me go flying into the bottles. By the look on her face when she came out of the store, she wasn't very happy about the results. Served her right. Something told me that she was being punished by having to pay for the damage she caused by shoving me head-first into the bottles. I wonder how many green stamps that took to pay off!

When we got home, I was awaiting the inevitable as I sat on the kitchen floor, putting the cans in the cabinet. When the final bag was set down, Elaine started in with her scolding only to be interrupted. Instead, I heard Hank stick up for me and tell her straight out that she couldn't take it out on me, and that it wasn't my fault. What a strange turn of events that was! This was reminiscent of the days when Cindy and I would take off running after getting beat, Hank coming after us, stepping in and trying to do the right thing. It seemed that he was doing so again, trying to do the right thing.

These types of mixed messages continued to confuse my understanding of affection. Just a few weeks before, I was being yanked out of bed in the middle of the night by an intoxicated bully. Now transformed, he comes to my rescue and stands up, in rare fashion, to Elaine. With my eyes straight ahead, I listened silently. None of it made any sense.

~.~.~.~

When school started up again I continued where I had left off the year before. On the first day I made a point of watching where Karen, the girl I took the homework from, would decide to sit. I simply grabbed the seat in front of her so I would have access to her homework. Although I did not sit at the front of the row, I was still positioned so that, when the papers came forward, I could intercept hers, cross her name out and write mine in. The only problem was that we soon switched to pencils and the red crayon mark looked out of place. I made it through about three months before getting caught.

Mrs. White was an older, pleasant lady with white hair. She called me up at the end of class one day to ask me about the red scribble at the top of my paper. I told her I didn't know why I did it but I just did and shrugged my shoulders. Then, to my surprise, she reached in her drawer and retrieved a big pair of metal scissors, opened them up and took the sharp side of the blade and scraped the crayon off, revealing the girls name underneath. Needless to say, I was in big trouble.

There I was, the first second grader in history to get kicked out of Wilson Elementary for cheating. I had been doing it all the way through first grade and the fact that I had gotten away with it for so long didn't help matters. The principal met with Mrs. White, Elaine and me and when asked how all this started, I must have really shocked them when I shared the whole story. That was my last day at Wilson Elementary.

Foundation of Support

Hank was good at putting down the neighbors across the street. Just "dumb Mexicans," He would say. "All he does is cement because he is too stupid to get a better job."

Even at this young age, I understood that his put downs were intended to make himself feel more superior.

Funny how things work out. About a week after getting kicked out of Wilson, I was being baptized Catholic by those same neighbors. Mr. and Mrs. Lucio stepped up and baptized me, making it possible to attend Our Lady of the Pillar, a Catholic school just south of us. They also became one of my first guiding lights in life.

This event impacted my life dramatically. As I stood in front of the alter awaiting my turn, I gazed at the stained glass illuminated by the morning sun. Standing next to me were my sponsors, the nice man from across the street that always gave me that knowing look and smiled at me with a small wave. His wife stood on my other side. They both walked me up and claimed me in front of the church full of strangers. Being supported as my head tilted back and the water rolled off my forehead, a feeling spread through me, starting in my chest and moving into my stomach. My entire upper body felt like a million little fire flies and I was filled with this warming sensation.

As my feet found the floor and my head came forward, my eyes were met by so many warm smiles, welcoming me into the Catholic Church.

Immediately there was a noticeable difference in the blatant mistreatment from Elaine and Hank. Perhaps the thought of other eyes watching had them thinking – although I felt there had been eyes watching for a long time. The beatings that, at one time, sent us running down the street seemed to subside completely, as did many of the abusive actions that took place in front of others.

The next day I started parochial school. I'm not sure why, but I was put back into the first grade and my work was monitored daily by Hank or Elaine. I liked my teacher, who happened to be a nun. She was nice and very kind and she inspired me. My grades were solid and I strived to be a good student, proudly carrying my briefcase back and forth from school. I felt important, like I had purpose as I walked.

The classroom was structured, well organized and smelled clean with spotless floors and desks that were polished. We wore uniforms and followed strict rules, instilling a common thread of equality, separated only by our individual features above the buttoned up white shirts and red bow ties.

Although I was one of the few white kids, I felt no racial overtones. This contrasted sharply with my memories of Wilson where most everyone was white as was the neighborhood. This, too, lent understanding of the social standards of the times.

Walking south down Raitt Street was like entering the forest. The edge was groomed and fresh looking, inviting. But, as I continued south passing Fremont, the elementary school that rested on the corner of Civic Center and Raitt, I began to see the dead woods of an old neighborhood: homes lacking plaster exteriors or manicured lawns. Instead, the wood sidings were weathered and the yards were balding with patches of dirt. There were porches filled with potted plants tended to by elderly women that shared their homes with extended family, enlightening me to the cultural differences of one race compared to another.

As a white kid, one of the few, I learned a valuable lesson. In contrast to Wilson, where most of the kids were white, the homes were newer, and the neighborhood was nicer, I could feel and see a difference as I walked through this older, poorer neighborhood toward my new school.

Our Lady was laid out differently than Wilson, as the building started with the first grade classroom at one end and wrapped all the way around to the eighth grade class next to the principal's office. The principal, also a nun, was very important. Everyone respected her and showed reverence when she came out during recess.

Her long string of beads made a belt and hung almost to the ground. They rattled in cadence with her steps as she walked, and she was always

accompanied by two other nuns, one on each side. The sight of her demanded respect and everyone acknowledged her as the matriarch of this big
family where all were treated warmly.

Each morning I would walk by myself down Raitt Street, south toward Fifth Street before heading east. On that corner was the feed store and
the scent of various pet supplies filled the air as I approached. Taking a quick
glance in, or sometimes a brief stop, I would check to see if there were any
new baby chicks under the bright yellow lights of the pen.

Occasionally, I would stop at the small neighborhood store and cash
in the few soda bottles I had gathered along the way, enough to buy a pack-
age of caramels. This would get me through the morning until lunch where
I would pull out a peanut butter sandwich, made the night before. Peanut
butter seemed to still be my staple except, of course on Thursdays, when the
whole school got hamburgers.

Thursdays were my favorite because you could smell the hamburgers cooking all morning. They were only served that day and they were free;
a welcoming treat to my hungry tummy. At lunch time, everyone would go
into the dining hall and get their hamburger and milk. Our class went first.
We would come from the church a few minutes early and were seated before
the rest of the grades were led in. We all wore uniforms and the rules were
very strict, yet it all made sense to me as a harmonic energy buzzed about the

room. There was a certain rhyme to the reason as I observed a sea of white shirts and red sweaters monitored by several nuns throughout the giant hall.

~.~.~.~

Hank and Elaine weren't by any means poor. They were middle class and Hank worked long hours driving trucks. Elaine now worked evenings and they also received money from the State for taking care of us. At Christmas, the tree – a white artificial aluminum – would be loaded solid all the way around with all kinds of presents. Most of the time whatever Roberta opened, there would be an identical gift for Cindy and the same went for little Henry and me. Elaine orchestrated the sequence of the presents, making sure Cindy and I always went after Roberta or little Henry and that we opened the exact presents they did.

After opening up the gifts Hank would usually say, "Kids, to me Christmas is *every* day." It was his way of saying he had done his best. Actually, when compared to other kids, Elaine and Hank went overboard with presents under the tree.

Although they had given us all these presents, they could see how sad Cindy and I were. We were lonely and didn't feel loved. We knew too well there was a double standard and no amount of presents would ever change that. When we were all done opening up our gifts it was I who fetched the trashcan for all the wrappings, and Cindy who fetched Elaine a refill for her coffee.

This Christmas, I got a new Stingray bicycle. Hank was anxious for me to ride so we went out front where he put me on it and gave me a small shove. I had never ridden a two wheeler and Hank was determined that I would learn without the assistance of training wheels. Several attempts later, it was no longer fun as Hank was losing his temper and becoming impatient. With the neighbors watching, he was determined to show off and decided to give me a running shove into the street and, as he did, I went across the drive and up the edge of the apron, off the curb and fell over into the street.

As I hit my head on the cement surface, a car drove past and I could hear and feel the whisk of wind from its tire right next to my head. The look in Hank's eyes confirmed how close the car had come. He was scared and re-alized I could have been killed. He took the bike and put training wheels on as I sat on the steps thinking about what had just happened. I felt an internal alarm, the rush of adrenaline throughout my body as I tried to calm the jitters causing me to shake.

I knew his short temper was fused to his impatient actions. That is why he forced the issue, thinking if he tossed me out of the nest I would have to fly. Instead, I fell to the ground, narrowly escaping injury.

This wouldn't be the last time he forced the issue. He used the same tactic the following summer in his attempt to teach me to swim. Frustrated with my inability to float on my back, like he could, the sessions would end. Then came the day he called for me to come out back to swim. Doing as I was told, I changed into my suit and went out the back door, up the steps to the sun deck he had built the day before. Expecting another floating lesson, I walked across the deck, noticing he was dressed in street clothes. Soon it became clear, as he picked me up and said, "Sink or swim," and tossed me like a sack of potatoes into the pool.

The sensation of panic filled my chest as I belly flopped into the pool, feeling the burn on my tummy as my mouth filled with water. I pushed myself off the bottom of the vinyl lining toward the surface gulping for air and splashing toward the side wall of the above ground swimming pool until I grasped the side and held on.

I looked up to the deck without a clue as to why he had done that. He just stood there, hands on his hips, grinning with satisfaction. "See, you're alright. I knew you could do it!"

I had passed this test of his. He wanted to make sure that if I ever fell in I could make it to the side. I wondered what his point was but, moreover, I found a new fear of him. I would never trust him again. His concept of teaching by force was archaic, even by the standards of a seven year old.

Defining the Moments

~.~.~.~

In August of 1965, a buzz resonated in the air along with random sirens that started in the distance and rolled toward our home. On their porches were all the grown ups, and many of the men were armed as they stood. My uncle, too, stood at the top of the steps, united in cause as the first of three cruisers zipped by our house with the sirens blaring.

Standing there observing, my eyes scanned down the street to see where they would go. At the corner, they stopped to create a barricade that directed a group of marchers toward El Salvador Park.

Turning on the television, my uncle tuned into a news broadcast that said, "Los Angeles on fire." An area they called Watts was rioting. I had no idea what this was all about other than my uncle saying that the "niggers" were torching and looting their own city. It wasn't the first time I had heard that word, but it still sounded vile. He and my aunt went on and all the words in the air were about "niggers." As they talked, their anger filled the room and for the first time their rage was not directed toward me or my sister. They were angry about the pictures on the RCA that flickered while Hank's hands were on the rabbit ears trying to clear the vertical roll.

This urgency of the situation had nothing to do with the house we lived in or my sister and I. I continued to absorb entirely different feelings associated with raised voices. These voices were frightened by the unknown. I knew this fright and had felt it many times in this home. Now, what I saw told me they were scared.

In the distance, the sound of more sirens filled the air, but they weren't coming here. They were going away from us, further south. The lumber yard was now on fire and burned just a handful of blocks away from us near my school. As the sirens eventually turned off, the blaze took its turn in the night air, filling it with the smell of a giant bonfire. Ashes and embers fell about the neighborhood. For days, the talk was about how windows were broken and vandals looted everything in demonstration and support of what was happening in Watts.

A few weeks later I would walk down the same street the demonstrators had. Although I saw no broken windows or signs of violence, the night before my uncle had warned me stay away from anyone I saw that was black. Safely, I made it to school without incident. Within a few days the apprehension that lingered from the activities weeks before was gone. I saw no danger and felt no threat as I walked to and from school.

My second year at Our Lady of the Pillar was very different from the first grade. Instead of a nun, we had a Filipino woman who lacked the graces of the teacher that led our class the year before. She was mean spirited and yelled when angry which seemed to be constantly.

Ms. Motas terrified us all. She reminded me of Elaine by the way she yelled, and would look at you intending to intimidate as she walked about teaching the lesson. Adding to that, she spoke with a dialect that amplified the difficulty of learning. Each day during recess, the kids from my class would talk about their dislike for her.

She had a habit of eating apples during class. With a straight-edged razor she sliced the apple and brought it to her lips, laying the fruit on her tongue, then slowly removing the blade from her mouth. At times she would be angry and yelling with that knife in her open hand. I couldn't help but wonder if she was ever going to use it. As she would yell, she would wave the blade up and down just inches from your face causing you to lean back away from her. Although she did not yell at me often, the sight of this still scared me.

She also used the ruler across the top of our knuckles. This wasn't uncommon, however, because the nuns also did this when deserved. The worst thing about Ms. Motas was the way she pulled your ears. This was absolutely mean and uncalled for. She would get so angry and yell at you, not for being bad but for not understanding or being able to answer a question. Sometimes she would grab and twist your ear so hard that tears would begin to fall.

This alarmed me as I identified with abuse and anger. I had learned to love to be at school when I came over in the 1st grade, but now I did not like the way it felt and, again, I started to lose my interest, shutting down and tuning out. I couldn't wait for the end of the day, just to get away. My peaceful time was now limited to the streets as I walked to and from school. It was the only place I didn't worry about getting in trouble.

Home life was gradually slipping back into the old routine. The newness of changing schools had worn off and, as autumn filled the air, the sun set earlier and I found myself confined to the inside of those white walls until bedtime.

The girls were now in Willard Junior High and Cindy consumed herself with glee club and orchestra as well as other school functions whenever possible. This allowed her the opportunity to get out of the house, however, the treatment she weathered still remained brutal as several times a week, she would be beaten and slapped around by Elaine.

Wearing a retainer in her mouth to curb an overbite, our aunt would order her to remove it so it wouldn't get broken while she would get the crap beaten out of her. Literally amazing were her words, "I'm going to beat the shit out of you so take out that retainer, God damn it!" Cindy would take it out and lay it carefully upon the kitchen counter and, if she had on her glasses, she would take them off as well, standing tall and taking her beating. She would calmly rinse it off before placing it back into her mouth.

Elaine empowered herself upon my sister, seeming to relish beating her as she stood in defiance with only soft tears of frustration rolling from her eyes. Speaking soundlessly, these vessels carried a cargo of heartfelt pain, an overload from the countless times she gathered her soul and tucked it away tightly, barely salvaging what was left for another day.

As we became older, jealousy and resentment grew between Cindy and Roberta. It seemed as if Elaine did everything she possible could to level the playing field. However, her attempt to hold Cindy down lost steam as my sister's theatrical talents blossomed along with her singing, forging a refuge of inner strength, a barrier that protected her spiritual awakening; separating her from the physical and actual, allowing her to escape into her own sacred place.

Roberta continued to struggle with her size. Not learning the value of self hygiene, she continually harbored greasy hair, pimples, grungy teeth and bad manners. Grandma Whitsett once told me one of the reasons she never invited Roberta over was because she couldn't stand to look at her, and that she ate with her hands like an animal. From this contempt I learned compassion. I knew she would be doomed to struggle socially, for she in her own way would suffer a different kind of abuse, but without the same intent Cindy and I knew. This abuse crippled her ability to adjust and conform independent from her mother.

Cindy was getting attention from boys at school and was becoming very popular. Being pretty and having lots of friends and an unleashed spirit (when away from the house) she attracted many. Nevertheless, as opposite as could be, the two of them did many things together, slowly finding a common ground of understanding.

As time went on, we were permitted to join the rest of the family in watching television on Sunday nights when Bonanza and Walt Disney's Wonderful World of Color or the Wild Animal Kingdom would come on.

On this one night, Disney's Cinderella was featured and my sister and I were amazed how the story related so much to us. Really, it applied more to Cindy because of the Roberta aspect but, later on, in a few years, I would become a Cinderella in my own way.

Cindy's ability to remember words from the songs of the movie carried her through her lonely times. As she worked about, staying busy with her chores around the house, she filled the air with the whimsical tunes and danced through the rooms, literally whistling while she worked.

She had found an inner peace in this place. With her soul tucked safely away, she lifted her voice for all to hear. Even Elaine, on occasion, sat in silence, listening to the beautiful voice rolling throughout the house, Cindy singing loud and clear with deep feelings.

On the weekends, or if school was out of session, the kids in the neighborhood gathered on the steps of the house or in Nellie's driveway just to hear as her words flowed through the windows or open door.

Perhaps Cindy's safe place was her mind, filled with fantasies that allowed her to escape the painful path she was forced to endure. She actually believed her mother was the same Dorothy from the Wizard of Oz. The farmhouse reminded us of Georgia and the wicked old witch on her bicycle, peddling to outrun the twister, reminded us that good will always prevail over evil.

Cindy always believed our mother would be coming for us one day but, as the years passed, her hopes faded and we realized the person she called "our mother" would not be coming soon. This was harder for her than me as Cindy once lived with her mother and had a face to attach to the memories. As for me, I only had dreams of how she might look. Still, I believed that destiny would one day bring us in touch and our mother would re-enter our lives. I always felt destined that I would someday meet both of my parents.

My Spiritual Place In The Streets

For me, I was drawn toward the neighborhood in the direction of the park. On the path to school, I came across a special place that I found my-self passing almost everyday. It was only a handful of houses down toward the west and in front of a vacant lot. There sat three amazing trees: the kind that dropped large long brown pods during the fall and winter months. It seemed each day as I ran down the street toward Raitt, I would feel an amaz-ing energy come over me when I passed under these trees. Many times, I would stop in the center of them to feel the sensation consume me. Eventu-ally the energy I felt dictated a ritual of honor that became sacred to me.

As I approached the edge of the great canopy I would stop, then slow-ly walk, letting my body be filled by an invisible power, reaching that warm special place we all have inside. Once I passed under and reached the other side, I would resume my fast pace, running toward my destination.

One particular day, as I was walking home from school, my mind began to wonder about thoughts of who my mother might be. Approaching these sacred trees, I stopped and, for a moment, I gazed at the majestic vi-sual they offered towering above so very powerful. I then continued until I reached the western edge of the canopy. I walked slowly, feeling each step and, as the sun warmed my back and shoulders, my mind filled with a vision.

It was of a lady with red hair that was long and full of body, flowing slightly past her shoulders. She was slim but stood tall and had beauty resembling that of a movie star.

Stopping in the center, I was compelled to turn around and, as I did, standing on the corner of Raitt and 9th was a lady with the same color red hair I had envisioned. We made eye contact even though we were at a distance and, as we did, I felt a sense connecting us for that moment. I felt her goodness, like that of a guardian strategically placed, purposely trying to send me a message.

Although I saw her many more times – and she saw me – we never spoke, but I wondered if maybe she was my mother. This is when I first felt a need to know who my mother was. I had a need to know who I was. I had met my grandmother and grandfather on my mother's side, as well as some uncles and aunts, but I still needed to know.

My grandfather Hansen was a quiet man and kept to himself. His house was peaceful and neat and smelled good. The air was always filled with the richness of his pipe or a cigar slowly burning near by. He once gave to me an empty cigar box, a King Edward's with an attached lid. I treasured it and kept it as my secret box where only special marbles and bubblegum could be stashed.

Occasionally I would visit my grandparents, spending the day exploring and doing various things with my uncle Chris who was seven years older than me. Their house was surrounded by orange groves and eucalyptus trees. It seemed like acres of forest were just at the edge of the backyard and, as we would explore we would hunt for snakes and other wildlife. Turning over old stumps we were trying to find rattlesnakes but seldom did we find anything more than lizards or a few worms.

Uncle Chris had pigeons and a chicken coupe. Next to the coupe, he had built a fort where he would sometimes sleep overnight. Once, when I was very young, I tried to spend the night in there but, shortly after dark, I became scared and grandpa brought me into the house.

Other times when I stayed with him I would lay on the bear rug in the living room at his feet. It was huge and the teeth were large, with glass eyes and stiff hair that felt good on my skin. Grandpa would sit in his chair and read while he smoked his pipe. I would lay on the floor next to him, just happy to be there.

Grandpa did most of the cooking. We would peel potatoes together and talk while the water boiled. He could peel a whole potato perfectly from start to finish without breaking the skin. He would then take the whole mess and make mashed potatoes for dinner. Everything he cooked seemed wonderful and we all would eat at a big dining room table that was set perfectly with silver and napkins. This was such a contrast to the way things were at my aunt's house.

Grandpa died at the young age of fifty eight. I was very sad when I heard the news. Being so young, Elaine did not let me attend the funeral. This was especially hard on me because Grandpa Whitsett had died just a year or so earlier. When Grandpa Hansen died, Hank said the strangest thing about it being alright to feel sad because he was my real grandpa. He was comparing Grandpa Hansen to Grandpa Whitsett. I guess he was saying I shouldn't have felt bad when grandpa Whitsett died, but I did and, to this day, I remember him fondly.

Uncle Chris was now by himself with Grandma. I felt sad that he didn't have his father anymore. I knew he had a big heart and would miss his dad. They were close and Chris was the youngest of seven children. I will never forget when I got the chicken pox how he rode his bicycle all the way, about five miles, to Elaine's house to see me and bring me a bag full of bubblegum. What he did was something very special for me and I loved him for it.

~.~.~.~

I was allowed to participate in little league as the result of my new Godparents who lived across the street. Mr. Lucio had two boys and managed one of the teams at El Salvador, the park at the end of Ninth Street where we lived. They put pressure on Elaine, appealing to her that it would be good for me and I would meet other kids, and that baseball was very important for boys. Remembering back, Elaine and Hank both made a point to inform me that this was a privilege and that it would be taken away if I did something wrong or got into trouble. I can't tell you how many times they would punish me and take away my sports activities for seemingly no reason.

I was on the Orioles and my coach was Mr. Giagos who worked at the Sugar Factory. He had three boys of his own, two of whom were on the team. This was a wonderful experience for me as it gave me something to do and fostered a sense of belonging. Mostly I played center field my first year but occasionally I would get moved onto second base. I was small and that meant I would draw a walk because I had, literally, no strike zone. I was the "Bad News Bears" version of the little kid whose back pockets literally hung down to the back of his knees.

Empowerment In The Streets

Sometimes walking home could be rough. I was small and there were some pretty tough kids in the neighborhood. Also, being white, I stood out, especially in the park. Mostly black and Hispanic kids hung out at El Salvador. The older kids ran in small gangs – usually five or more at a time. This could be a problem but, mostly, they didn't mess with young kids like me.

One day, I was leaving the park after a Saturday game. As I walked from the fields toward Raitt Street, I felt the presence of danger around me. Soon, a group of older kids came from around the corner of the rec center and I realized they were a gang of Chicano teenagers. From across the park, they observed me as I continued, trying my best to ignore their stares. In no time, they started toward me and I knew they were going to give me trouble. Knowing I could not run from them I realized I would have to face whatever was coming.

As they approached me they called me names and tried to intimidate me. Instinctively, I felt the danger and knew I could not show them I was afraid. Two of the kids pulled out their stiletto knives and started taunting me with them.

I didn't say anything, but I looked them right in their eyes as I kept walking. After shadowing me for a minute or so, they started playing chicken with me by throwing their knives at my feet.

One would throw his knife and it would land inches in front of my foot. I would keep walking without breaking my stride and then another would throw his knife and it would land even closer. They would make cracks about sticking me and I would look at them all the while, right into their eyes. After the fourth one tossed his knife, the bigger one, who must have been the leader and who I never broke eye contact with, pushed his knife back into the handle and said to the others, "Let's go." I could tell he felt stupid.

Here was a little kid, small for his age and only eight anyway, who wasn't afraid of them or, at least, was unwilling to show his fear. The leader sensed that I knew what he was all about and he was right. I had been getting kicked around now for the last five years and there was nothing that could have made me tougher. They couldn't hurt me and I was ready to fight if I had to.

As they walked away, the leader kept looking back at me with a puzzled expression. Finally, he gave me a nod of approval and a slight smile. I had connected with him and that was a good thing. He must have been well known because, from that point on, other kids showed me respect. Once in a while I would see him and he would give me that nod. I was accepted now and this incident, although frightening, would change my outlook on street life.

The lesson I learned – another defining moment – was the value of standing my ground and showing pride. In the street, some act like animals, preying on the weak to satisfy their hunger for acknowledgment or to belong. Some are bullies while others are bullied, but I would be neither. I made a stand in the face of true danger and racial tension and came out on the better end for it. I realized there is a difference between small vs. weak. Later in life I heard the saying:

"It's not the size of the dog in the fight; it's the size of the fight in the dog."

Learning To Take The Wall

The summer was nearly over and I would soon be starting the third grade. My birthday was September 11th and it seemed to always land on the first day of school. Happy to have a nun again, I enjoyed being back in school as the classroom felt friendlier than it did the year before.

The days were rather boring at first, with not much in the way of new events. Although I had friends I was still very much a loner and did not participate with others. I spent most of the time during recess on the swing or, if they were full, I would just sit on a lunch table by myself. The other kids, although they were mostly friendly and treated me nice, left me alone. This one kid named George, who was popular and also one of the bigger kids, talked to me sometimes asking me what was wrong. It was as if he seemed to sense that my life was different and he wanted to understand. Mostly he would talk and I would just nod my head.

As we aged, we kids were getting bolder, and while I was no exception, I would maintain a shyness about me during school. My boldness came out outside of school, around the neighborhood and *certainly* on the walk home. I carried a ton of grief and did not like to be messed with. Although I was always polite, I had a way about myself that warned others to treat me with respect.

In late autumn, another defining moment was laid upon me. It was a Saturday morning, about eleven o'clock, the sun was bright and the sky was very clear. I was sent out to retrieve something for my uncle, so I went out the side door and headed toward the garage. Our neighbor, Sheila, was visiting, having a cup of coffee with Elaine while Hank worked on something in the kitchen.

Returning with his request, I could hear he had lost his temper and was in a fit of rage, for what I would never know. What I *did* know was that a man of 260 pounds could do a lot of damage to a kid of only eight years. I couldn't get through the one door, so I went around and came in through the front. Approaching the kitchen, I could tell he was angry as he stood with fire in his eyes glaring toward me. "Where the hell have you been, God damn it?!"

With that, he punched me in the face so hard that I literally flew into the wall across the room several feet away. He then kicked me as I was laying there with my back toward him and blood pouring from my nose. I didn't see it coming and it felt crushing as his shoe lifted me again into the wall.

Sheila stared in disbelief. She came over and helped me up to a chair while Elaine calmed Hank down. Leaving for a brief moment, Sheila returned with a washcloth and cleaned my face until the blood stopped flowing from my nose. I could hardly breathe as my ribs hurt from being kicked and my head swelled where it had hit the wall.

My eyes began to well up, but not from being hurt: from the feeling that someone actually cared enough to hold me and clean me up. I hadn't been held like this ever before and I had not known affection from anyone other than Cindy. Still, it wasn't like this.

I drew deep down to hold back my tears, as I did not want her to see me cry. I was afraid to show her my emotion, as I had never allowed them to be seen and, despite the tears in her eyes, I held mine back.

Something would happen months later that made me glad that I did.

The Custody Battle

Christmas vacation came and my uncle Ed, Elaine's brother, had asked if Cindy and I could come to visit with him and his family. This was not easily welcomed because Elaine wanted him to also invite Roberta and little Henry and felt he was giving us attention that she did not want us to have. Eventually, however, she agreed and he came to pick us up.

After a brief visit, we all left for his house in Corona. The city of Corona was a small town about twenty five miles east of Santa Ana. It was very rural with mostly farmhouses or small ranches.

Uncle Ed had a horse he allowed me to ride so I walked him over to a fence where I could hold his bridle as I climbed up the rails and onto his back. This is how I spent time during the day while he was off at work. It was very boring during these days at his house as, other than riding the horse, there was little else for me to do. My uncle also had some carving knives I would work with sometimes, mostly creating nothing, just keeping busy. I spent a lot of time walking around playing with the dirt or collecting rocks and lizards. In the evenings, we would sit on his bed with him and his wife Nancy and play card games. I loved the attention and the conversation and I loved the way I felt so special. Both of them made me feel so comfortable.

They would ask me questions about Elaine and how Cindy and I were treated. Although they were doing the asking, it seemed like they already knew the answers. As it turned out, they did. Conducting an interview to verify their suspicions, as well as confirming the information they had already received from Cindy, was prudent before taking their action. I was sure they knew how terrible our life at the Whitsett's had been because, whenever we would see them, they were always very attentive and supportive.

Elaine's relationship with her brothers and sisters was strained. Although I did not know this prior to staying with my uncle, it was clear to me by the questions they asked and their body language in reaction to my answers. This could partly have to do with the age difference and the fact that Elaine was much older than the rest of the children. She was grandpa's favorite and, as the eldest of seven, she played the role of overseeing the younger ones. My uncle Ed really didn't know my mother since he was only four when she had left home at the age of fourteen. Chris was only a baby then. Aunt Bonnie, now a teenager, was only two or three when Dorothy, my mother, left so she had no real relationship with her either.

After leaving my uncle's house, Cindy and I went to stay with my grandmother in Tustin. Grandma Hansen was happy to see us and, right away, took us down to the drug store where she bought me a new ball. I spent hours in the driveway and backyard kicking the ball up into the air and catching it before it hit the ground. My uncle Chris didn't spend much time around the house any more. He was busy running around with his friends and doing the things that teenagers do. In the late afternoons he would show up and we would spend some time together, but he spent more time with Cindy. They were closer in age and therefore had more in common. In the evening she would hang out with them on the front porch while I would stay inside with grandma.

Soon it became apparent to me that something was up. My uncles and aunts, all of them with the exception of Elaine and Hank of course, came down to Grandma's and we all had a talk. My uncle Donald was there and I remember talking to him about how Hank would hit and kick me and he asked me if I would like him to go kick Hank back. I don't remember what I said, but I do remember them all being very angry with Hank and telling me I didn't have to worry because I wasn't going back there.

Happy to hear this, Cindy and I felt a great sense of relief. The rest of the day was spent planning out who would be responsible for handling the different affairs. Cindy and I were to be enrolled into school and Donald was to call Elaine and Hank and let them know we weren't coming back. That was a big deal and it didn't take long for Donald to lose his temper, so grandma took over on the phone, telling Elaine that we had a family meeting and that she wanted me and Cindy to stay with her. I was kept outside of the room, but I remember this was the first time I ever heard my grandma angry.

She was ready to fight for us and she was not the fighting type. She told Elaine not to come around and if it meant getting a lawyer she would.

I felt secure at Grandma's because it reminded me of the days in Georgia. I loved the way she would sing hymns as she walked about the house and how everything was in its place. Grandma's house was clean: no one left their dishes laying about for Cindy or me to pick up. She was a God-fearing woman with a great heart and she loved us dearly.

I got to sleep in the top bunk in Chris's room. Grandpa had built these bunk beds right into the wall. On the floor was linoleum that had the pattern of a race track. I played with little cars on the floor and pretended to race around the track against make-believe opponents. Everything in Grandma's was magical and I loved the smell of all the hardwoods throughout the house. Each drawer was full of mysteries and everything inside had a special story to go with it. I felt lucky to be there and never once did I miss Elaine, Hank, Roberta or little Henry.

The first day in my new school was interesting. I made friends and got lots of attention, and the school work was very different than what I was used to. For one thing, there was nothing religious, which was good. There was no confession booth to go into and make up a story about doing something wrong either. I used to do this at Our Lady of the Pillar because I thought I was supposed to have something to tell the priest, so I would just make up that I said a bad word or peeked during a test.

Recess was very social. When the bell rang we had no line to form, we could just take off, and that we did, running as fast as we could to grab a monkey bar or swing or play tag. There were no uniforms with a clean white shirt to worry about. We could wear T-shirts and tennis shoes and so what if we got a grass stain? At least there was grass to slide on!

I would walk through the orange groves each day on the way to school and check out all the sights. I had a special shortcut I took across someone's land that bordered the groves and, at a certain point, I would cruise right through the heart of the trees and come out across the street from the school. I had figured it out myself and, since there was no one to walk home with I had fun exploring. I found myself intrigued by all of the sights like the heat pots that burned through the night to keep the frost off the oranges.

Many of the kids came by bus and, each morning as I would pop out of the groves, the buses would be unloading and the kids would be walking up. One day a kid told me I wasn't supposed to cut through the groves but I didn't care and continued to do it any way.

I heard that a girl named Jenny liked me and we began to talk and hang out at recess. It wasn't long before rumors began to fly. We used to chase each other around and all her friends thought I was cute. I was the center of attention and everyone was interested in where I came from and who I was. I too was wondering the same.

Each day we had a time to "show and tell." Not a day went by that I didn't bring something from Grandma's house to share and, of course, everything had a mystical story to go with it. Everyone was amazed and it made me feel important to share these things with my class.

I was changing for the first time in six years and was not afraid. I was excited to belong and it felt good to come home. No longer oppressed, I was now able to speak what was on my mind.

Weeks had gone by since anyone had hit me and absolutely no one yelled at or intimidated me. I was in an entirely different world; a world that allowed and expected self expression; a happy world where people were positive and clean. This world motivated me and opened my mind to life's offerings and colors, to the variation of smiles and welcoming gestures. I felt like a rose that had just opened up to show the world its beauty and was consuming the warmth and sunshine that now surrounded my world. I was happy.

We finished the school year and, as summer started, we learned that Elaine had sought legal channels to gain official custody of Cindy and me. Grandma had been dealing with an attorney and, with the support of the rest of her children, she was prepared to do whatever she could to keep us with her. On occasion, a man would come to Grandma's and interview Cindy and me. He would ask us about our life at Elaine's and some of the specific instances of abuse. We would sit at the dinning room table and grandma would leave the room while he asked questions. Cindy would answer most of the time and I would nod my head in agreement.

Most of his questions involved the beatings and physical abuse, although none of his interview seemed in-depth. I don't remember going into real detail nor do I remember him asking us to. He must have concluded most of his information from speaking with my uncles and grandmother and possibly Cindy, but little from me as I was only nine years old.

A few weeks passed and we would have another interview where he would go over the same questions and verify his information. Again, I participated little and Cindy did most of the answering.

At last, the big day came when we had to go to court. The courthouse was in downtown Santa Ana about a twenty minute drive from Grandma's. We were all dressed up and I felt confident that we would be staying with our grandmother, as did everyone else. In the back of Grandma's '54 Chevy, I sat quietly. Cindy sat up front with grandma as we toodled our way to the courthouse, all the while listening to Cindy and grandma reassure each other that we would soon be finished with this ordeal. Cindy was so excited knowing that she would never have to go back to that terrible place.

I remember walking up to the courthouse steps, passing the old canon along the way. The building was big and made of brick as it sat on a large knoll of green grass. It looked powerful and important and so did the people that walked in and out the front doors.

During the trial, Elaine's attorney focused on my grandmother's inability to raise children into responsible adults. She pointed out how Donald, her brother had gone to jail for beating someone up with a baseball bat and that Ed had run-in's with the law over marijuana. Chris, who was only sixteen, had been busted with a joint and her sister, Bonnie, was pregnant and unmarried. Her other sister, Cinni, had been divorced and remarried. Cinni's husband, Vern, had been involved in an automobile accident where he was convicted of manslaughter and did jail time as a result.

She painted a picture of grandma, portraying her as a weak adult with no leadership and obviously unable to raise her own children, let alone be trusted to raise her grandchildren whose own mother, a unfit stripper who was never married herself, abandoned them. If not for Hank and Elaine, "These children would surely be in an orphanage," she said.

What stood out most about the trial was that Elaine could only muster up one character witness for herself: Sheila, the lady from down the street. Neither the neighbors from next door nor my godparents from across the street were there. No one within earshot came to testify on her behalf.

The lady who did come lied to the court about ever seeing me hit or abused. Sheila, the lady that brought me a washcloth to wash my face and stop the bleeding that took several minutes, who was crying *herself* as she held me. How could she lie for Elaine? How could she fail to be honest when she herself witnessed this with her own eyes and cried as she washed me up? She knew what kind of people they were yet she testified on their behalf and told the court that they were loving parents and did well in providing for us.

The judge seemed to be confused and, when I testified, he asked me if Elaine and Hank ever told me they loved me or showed me any affection. I replied, "Once in a blue moon," and the court busted out laughing. The judge then took me into his chambers and we talked but I did not tell him about the abuse, because I thought he knew.

Alone, I sit with this man in his private chambers. He's dressed in a black robe and I see the knot of his necktie poking out the top. Across from him, I sit in a wooden chair, his eyes are questioning as his head tilts to the right.

He seems confused as he ponders the question I wait to hear. He asks me about school, I fidget with my hands and feet as I answer.

Again he looks deeply at me. He asks about pets and I reply. Then he asks me if I am happy and I tell him yes, referring to now, not when I lived at the Whitsett's.

He heard what my uncles said; he heard what my grandmother said. Hank's own mother didn't come to support him. One would think there was a reason, and there was. The last time I had seen my Grandma Whitsett was the day that we stopped by to mow her lawn. We left without starting as he called his mother names and, respectively, they invited each other to, "Go to hell."

Cindy even testified that Hank had made inappropriate remarks to her about himself sexually and told the court in detail how she was whipped and beaten and terrified to be there.

After I returned to the courtroom, there was this very long break. The judge returned and we all stood and came to order. The judge ruled that Cindy should be allowed to stay with her grandmother; that because of her age, the fact that she was fourteen, she was old enough to make her own decisions and knew what she wanted.

Then the judge said I would have to return to Elaine and Hank; that I was too young and did not know what was best for me and that Elaine could provide better for me. He said the environment there would be healthier because it was more of a family setting and, because my grandmother was a widow, it would be hard for her to raise me, especially given her age and situation.

The courtroom broke out in a gasp then uproar. Cindy screamed and cried out loud saying she promised never to leave me. She ran over to me and grabbed a hold of me as we began to cry. Everyone was crying. The entire family had been brutally defaced in an arena filled with hatred and anger, cut so deep with wounds that most would never heal. I, too, would be wounded. We had been cast in the middle of a family battle and we could only watch as the bad side won. I didn't understand. Good and evil, right and wrong, how could this be happening?

There was now something else to burden me: the guilt of our promise. I truly regretted the pact we had made to each other. Cindy had the opportunity to be free, to be with grandma and to live a normal life but, for me, she would give all that up, return to Elaine's and face what proved to be a violent and hateful future. From then on, every time she was beaten, my heart would find a lower place to go.

No Fear

We were returned to the Whitsett's custody, and to the eeriness of seeing that house again. In the back of that blue Thunderbird, we sat with a feeling that was so uneasy, wondering what would happen once back behind closed doors. As Hank pulled into the driveway, ending the silent drive from the courthouse, I felt like a prisoner who had once escaped and was then returned.

As things worked out, shortly after the trial was over I began the fourth grade. My already descending spirit sank even lower as I stood frozen in the doorway of my new classroom. Returning to Our Lady of the Pillar, I found that the same teacher I had in the second grade had been transferred to the fourth grade. What a blow to my already devastated heart! Not only was home life miserable but *school* would be also! It was bad enough that I would never see my new friends from Tustin again, but add to that the boredom of my old school and this teacher who pulled ears, yelled and waved a straight-edged knife in your face as she peeled her apple.

This would not be fun.

Several questions were tossed at me as a result of my absence. Kids at school wanted to know where I was, what happened to me, where I went. This was difficult to explain so, mostly, I just avoided the questions as much as I could. Depressed, I spent most of my time away from everyone else. I always remember how George would approach me, asking what was wrong and how sometimes he would just give up because I would not answer. I felt sorry for myself and was so unhappy. I didn't even pack a lunch, so I would be without anything to eat. I truly just didn't care.

I was not motivated to do my homework or to participate in class. This, of course, led to problems with Ms. Motas that eventually meant red, sore ears for me.

Big mistake!

When my teacher began punishing me with a ruler across the knuckles or pulling my ears, I immediately made up my mind that I would not tolerate it. Of course, as a ten year old, there is little you can do but rebel or retract and, since I was already a recluse, I had only one option left: I rebelled!

The next day at school, I did something devious!

It was late September and the sun was bearing down from the east into the window of our classroom. I was intent on getting even for having my ears pulled and being treated in that manner, and imagined what I could do to make myself feel better.

Walking to the pencil sharpener, I felt the heat from the opened windows and I could see the fumes radiate off the black top as I gazed outside. It was then that the idea came to me.

I went back to my seat and, in the same sneaky way I had stolen the girl's paper in the first grade, I resorted to the enlistment of my crayons. Slowly, without anyone noticing, I peeled the paper from around the crayons and broke them in halves. Now, armed with a dozen or so pieces, I again made my way to that side of the room to sharpen my already-sharp pencil. Checking to see that no one was looking, I laid several pieces just outside on the windowsill. I then walked farther down the aisle and did this again until I had set my soon-to-be-realized-vandals to work.

Now, with three piles set in the sun, all I had to do was wait! It was no time at all before the crayons began to melt into each other and blend to form a messy goop on the windowsill. I watched the reactions of the other kids as they would pass by them and see the mess. Their eyes would widen and, before I knew it, everyone was aware of what I had done. Everyone except the teacher, that is.

When my teacher came back into the room after a brief conference, I waited with anticipation as she began walking about the room. Eventually, she went down the far aisle where she passed right by the piles of rainbow colored mess.

I thought she would continue to pass right by them, but then she turned to look outside and, when she did, she bent right down and put her face within inches of the mess. When she stood up and spun around, the entire class froze. The rage in her face was not something we had seen before!

She demanded to know who had done this, and, although we were all tightlipped, she continued with threats. Finally, one girl broke down and started crying. She gave me up, ratting me out.

Furious, the teacher came over to me and grabbed both my ears, pulling them so hard that they began to burn from where her nails dug in. Just as she was doing this, the bell rang and class was out for the rest of the day.

Finding Myself

Walking home from school that day, I put much thought into what had happened and pondered what I could do about it. I could not tell Elaine, she wouldn't understand. Cindy was busy with high school and learning how to drive, as was Roberta, who I wouldn't talk to anyway. Little Henry was a squeal, so I certainly couldn't talk to him. There was nobody. Again, I was on my own.

I had already figured out that my home life was abnormal. Clearly, I was beginning to understand this new basis for comparison. My horizon had been widened by exposure from my time in Tustin. My friends there had loving parents who were supportive and built confidence in them. Even my friends at school *here* were happy. They smiled and seemed to enjoy life. Not once did I ever see bruises or hear about them being beaten. They may have been spanked, but certainly never punched.

Something was wrong, outrageously so, and it all pointed to Elaine and Hank. The way they treated Cindy was opposite from that of Roberta. Little Henry was spoiled rotten and could get away with saying or doing any-thing. He would egg me on and then run to Elaine and laugh as she whipped me with the belt. It was a game to him and Elaine knew what was going on, but she also knew it built confidence in little Henry when she would come to his rescue. What she would come to find out in later years was that his confidence was completely superficial.

Here I was, walking home, determined not to put up with my ears being pulled and not knowing how to resolve this. I didn't want to mix the abuse from my home life with school, the place that once was my sanctuary. Bringing attention to me at home, well, I knew that was going to happen soon by the way school was going.

I did not want to be in school. I did not feel loved. I felt like a slave, ordered to work around the house without being appreciated for it. The weekends were spent working on cars with Hank, not knowing when I was going to catch one in the back of the head or nose, or a kick in the butt, or a slap upside the head. Having had a taste of how it should be when I was with my grandmother, I knew *for sure* that Elaine and Hank were downright mean.

Finally, it came to me the next morning on my way to school. I got a flash of something. As I walked to school, I decided to cut through the park. Of course, the park was in the opposite direction and I took my time cruising through it. From there, I traveled west on Civic Center – then called Eighth Street – up to Sullivan where someone had a bunch of farm animals and fruit trees. I then traveled down to Tiny Tim's market and just walked around.

Before I knew it, ten o'clock came around and I certainly wasn't going to school now. How would I explain being two hours late? For sure I would get my ears pulled.

So I kept on going, through the junkyards past the barking dogs. I even cut through the lumber yard at Fifth and Raitt, the one that had burned down a few years earlier. Then I went farther south toward Third and English where I followed the railroad tracks toward Consumer City, a large department store. I cruised through but didn't stay very long as I got the, "Shouldn't you be in school?" and "What are you doing here?" looks. I was beginning to enjoy this newfound power, a cat and mouse game that left me feeling in charge.

Watching the clocks as I would cruise through the different stores, I kept track of time so I could slip home before any kids from school could see me. It was a challenge that provided intrigue and entertainment. After being successful the first day, I realized that I would not have a note from Elaine if I went back. That gave me the perfect excuse to skip school again. And again. I added variables into my day. Sometimes I would hang out at the park, but I would ditch anyone who got close as I couldn't risk being discovered.

I learned several things about the street that went beyond my ten years. One day while at the park, an older black kid who had a bad reputation tried to corner me in the boys' room. I had stopped in to take a leak and he must have seen me and followed me in. I felt a strange feeling, like an internal alarm telling me there was danger. I didn't like the feeling and knew he was up to something that was no good. He stood about five feet behind me and I knew I was in trouble. When I finished and turned around I could see that he had pulled down his pants and was pointing to his private parts.

My mind was quick and I knew I had to get out of there. As I moved away from the urinal, I stepped to the left and, sure enough, he tried to block me so I put a move on him and bolted out the door. Outside my heart was pounding as I was scared, realizing the danger and how lucky I was to escape. I made sure to get right out into the open because he followed me and I didn't want to be near bushes or anything that could conceal me.

I got away from him quickly and knew all I needed was a few steps, because nobody could catch me now, not like the day when knives were thrown at my feet. Now I was faster and could cut right or left like a cheetah chasing a rabbit. There was no way he would catch me, and so he gave up once he realized he couldn't. He knew he was in trouble but I didn't snitch. That was something that I *never* did unless it involved Cindy. Then I would do whatever it took, not letting anyone say or do anything against her. From that point on, that kid stayed away from me. I wondered if he had ever cornered other kids like that. He was at least fourteen so it would be easy for him to take advantage of a ten year old and I didn't know many ten year olds who would have the guts – or strength – to defy him.

As time went on, I started taking matches from the house so I could smoke the cigarette butts I would find by the railroad tracks. It wasn't that I liked to smoke: it was more out of boredom and trying to keep busy. Feeling very independent, I viewed myself as a person who was really on their own. The butts I would sometimes find would be almost half a cigarette. I would look for a good one and light it up as I walked, which made me feel very grown up. Soon, I was taking cigarettes from Elaine's pack and saving them for the next day's adventure. I would plan my route so I could smoke and not be discovered. It was important to know if a car was coming before the driver could see me. If someone saw me they would probably call Elaine and that would be the end of my freedom.

One of my favorite hangouts was the bowling alley. I could walk in at one end and out the other and, even though people would see me, they wouldn't care. As time went on, I ventured into south Santa Ana, a mostly black neighborhood. I avoided anything that could get me caught.

It's amazing how educating the streets can be to a ten year old.

Back up on Eighth Street was the strangest thing. An old lady was in a rocking chair in a backyard. What was strange was that she was also in a cage. Seriously: she was in a chicken wire cage that was about eight feet high by eight feet wide. All day she would sit in that cage, just rocking away. It wasn't a screened in cage either, it was chicken wire! She must have been put in it each morning and taken out after the people got home from work. She had it pretty bad and I felt very sorry for her. A few times, I would stop and try to talk to her but she didn't speak back no matter what I tried. I remember comparing her to me and thinking she was really in a sad situation.

Some days my travels would take me down to the local Good Will. I would Cruise through the "as is" lot and cut though the store, but never stay long. I knew I had no excuse for being there and wanted to avoid getting asked why I wasn't in school. One of my other stops would be Angeles Quarries. It was a material yard that sold concrete and other things. I thought it was neat to see all that stuff and to watch the trucks go in and out.

I had become a pro at avoiding being caught. It had been several weeks since I was in school, time enough for me to realize that, sooner or later, I would be caught and would pay dearly for what I was doing.

It was about midmorning when I was at the park, looking past the parking lot down the street in the direction of our house that I saw Elaine backing out of the driveway. She was in her powder blue Thunderbird and was headed toward me. I quickly bolted across the grass to get out of sight, however, it was too late. She had gotten a glimpse of me and pulled into the parking lot. I had jumped behind an Oleander bush and was hiding, watching her as she hesitantly called for me. I stayed in hiding for about five minutes, listening to her talk to Cindy who was with her. She was saying, "I could have sworn I saw him running across the grass."

I knew I was busted and even if I stayed hiding, the jig was up. I could have stayed there but what about when I got home? She would be waiting, so what's the difference? I came out of hiding and called her. She was shocked beyond belief. She couldn't believe I had not been in school. Apparently, as fate would have it, she received a call from the school that morning and was on her way down to see where I was. The school thought I must have been at home sick and decided to call. They probably figured I was not coming back after what had happened with the custody battle the year before, explaining why they waited so long to call.

Elaine took me home, the belt came out and my pants came off. "Take off your God damn pants, you little bastard! I'm going to beat you within an inch of your life!" She beat me for what seemed like forever, leaving welts up and down my back from my shoulders to my knees. These welts swelled so much that the pores of my skin puffed with red dots. She even hit me in the face with the belt and grabbed me with her hand, digging her nails into my neck. She was intent on beating me just as she promised, "Within an inch of my life."

Although I was used to getting the belt, Elaine made sure this time was special. It was her intention to show me I could expect serious consequences when I did something that was bad and actually deserved punishment. She wanted to distinguish the difference between the normal everyday slaps, hits and beatings from how it would be when I really had it coming. As a result of moving away from the impact of the belt, I had several lashes hit me across the back of the head and in my face, even my ears.

This was not typical, but Elaine was furious and had lost all control of her temper. Her anger had consumed her as she wailed away, attacking with the intent to do more than just make me think. She wanted to physically hurt me and this she did. When she was finished, I was not able to walk to my room. I literally *crawled* down the hall and onto the bed. Like a wounded animal I spent the next couple days just lying in a ball.

For the first of many times, I think about the gun in my uncle's top drawer and the clip lying next to it. What if I was to get his gun and just end this pain? No, not that way. I will find the strength to carry on. There will be a way to show them my pain without hurting myself, I think as the idea fades.

The Pecking Order

The following week I was enrolled into Fremont, the elementary school around the corner. Although Elaine did not want me to attend this school, because its students were mostly Mexican and black, she simply had no choice. Expelled from Our Lady and Wilson, there was no other place left.

Fremont was an older school, overcrowded and known for its violence. I was familiar with the reputation the school carried and knew it was tough, but that didn't matter to me. I was excited to finally be with the kids I knew from the park and baseball.

Now ten, I was beginning to come into my own. I had missed much of the last baseball season due to the custody battle, so some time had passed since I had seen many of these kids. A lot can change in a year, and returning to a street environment opened up dynamics new to me. No doubt the time I had recently spent cutting school and cruising the surrounding streets would result in helping me prepare for the changes I would soon experience.

Although I wanted to be friends with everyone, I soon found this was just not possible. The rules of the street prohibited neutrality. Choices would have to be made and that included claiming your friends.

The play ground was a rough place that continually served as an arena for the ongoing and constantly changing pecking order. There were several fights a week during recess, however most of the really violent stuff went on after school on the streets and it generally involved more than fists.

Each recess, all of us boys would head out to the field and teams would be chosen for the various games. In the fourth grade we weren't allowed to play football because of our size, so most of us would play kick-ball. Being the new kid, I was chosen last and my welcoming to the group was less than friendly. It seemed like I would be an outcast despite the few familiar faces.

Shortly after the game began, my turn came to be up. As I approached home base preparing to kick the ball, I was stopped by a kid much larger than me and told I couldn't have my turn. He pressed up against me, bumping me back as some of the other kids laughed. I stood there in dismay, without a clue what I was supposed to do. I soon realized this was just the set up to start a fight with me, something I had not yet been involved in.

I had done nothing to provoke this, yet I found myself being con-fronted and immediately realized just how rough this school was going to be. This boy, who was much bigger than me, got in my face and forced the issue. I knew I would have to fight back and prepared myself mentally for what was going to happen. Suddenly, another boy about his size stepped up between us, popped him, and told him to leave me alone. The bully backed down and left the area.

The next day a similar thing happened. Again at recess another kid tried to start a fight with me. This time, though, he wanted to let me know that no one was coming to my rescue. With a serious look on his face, he told me he could kick the kid's butt that stood up for me yesterday. Looking over, the kid who stood up for me the day before was there and confirmed he was no match for this bully. Clearly, I was on my own.

With more kids gathering, the crowd began to grow, getting larger by the second. I stood there in the midst of this group, wondering why this was happening. With no options left, I readied myself to fight back. That's when someone suggested we take it to the park after school.

When you went to the park to fight, you could expect more than just a fist fight. It could mean two or three on one. Although I was concerned, I felt that I had to prove myself or this would never stop and I would become a target for everybody to pick on. I stood up for myself and agreed to go to the park after school.

Sitting in class that afternoon, I felt the eyes of others on me. Little comments about this kid's reputation, and how he was known for beating up others slipped past my ears as the drama of it all set in. When the bell rang everyone poured out of the building and I found myself surrounded by a wave of bodies that were there to witness the spectacle. One black girl, Kim, who was bigger and tougher than many of the boys was acting as the ring leader. She was talking trash as we marched, with racial overtones that insinuated the white boy she had dubbed "egg head" – me – was going to get his ass kicked.

Although I felt the odds were against me, I knew I had to go through with it or I would deal with this wherever I went. As we walked, cutting mid block across Civic Center, the crowd continued to grow. Passing the corner market, I realized there was no way out of this. That's when this strange sense began to come over me. I felt as though I was in a cloud of people, literally floating to the park like a warrior. In front marched this menace, intent on proving he was tough. In the midst of this cloud was me, being herded like a stray calf to be slaughtered by the giant. Toward the arena under the massive trees at the far corner we headed, crossing the grass as we went.

It took a good five minutes to get to the park under the big oak trees and form a huge circle. The kids were all around us as we got ready to start. The bully was eager to go, but what he didn't realize was that I was not afraid. I might feel pain, but I was used to that from Hank and Elaine, and I knew by that feeling that came over me during our march that I would be okay: he could not hurt me. After all, there wasn't a kid alive that could punch harder than Hank. Since I was three, I had weathered his wrath and the feeling in my chest grew even stronger as I realized there was *no way* this kid was going to win.

As the fight began the bully came up and shoved me, and I pushed him back. He then threw a punch that missed. I swung back and hit him on the side of his head, then tackled him while he was off balance. Grabbing hold of his legs I lifted him, maintaining my grip as he fell. I then turned him onto his neck, pinning him upside down while I still had my feet. He started screaming from the pain as his neck twisted against the grass, and then he started to cry. I kept my hold for a bit longer and all the while he cried out for me to stop.

When I finally let go and jumped off, he stayed on the ground curled in a ball, crying. Stepping back, I observed the shocked looks. They came to witness the white boy get his ass kicked by the bully, but what happened was just the opposite. At that instant, I gained recognition and respect. Everyone now knew I wasn't a push over and would not back down, even though I was much smaller than most. It felt great to be the victor, like David after he whipped Goliath.

Although this incident started out as the classic bully story – not so different than what many kids face growing up – it had a very unexpected element. This was a total and absolute victory for the underdog with results that changed my outlook at a very young age. I was one of the few white kids now running in that part of the 'hood. Regardless of what my color may have been going into this situation, coming out, it meant nothing.

I was now one of them and, though we had different skin tones, I blended in becoming part of the 'hood,' accepted by all. Respect came from the toughest, some of whom would later die in gang violence and other consequences, a part of life in the neighborhood.

My outlook on home life was also impacted. While I had grown to know I could handle the brutality of beatings, what I struggled to understand was the verbal and emotional abuse. The constant remarks about my intelligence – Hank referred to me as an "ignoramus," while Elaine called me a "little bastard" daily and reminded me how my father was a thief and how I would surely become the same. All these words led to one fact: that I was inferior by their standards, less than an equal. The same feelings of discrimination that rippled through me that first day in Fremont hit home as well.

I wanted so badly to please them yet I didn't know how nor did I know how to show them I was more than they ever gave me credit for. Now the attention I lacked at home would be supplemented by my life as a kid in the street, learning the street and acting like the street. There I would unleash the character that was stifled inside those white walls, though the attitude I learned would eventually separate me into two very different personalities.

~.~.~.~

Christmas that year also contrasted from those that came before. As though they wanted to make up for last year when we were away at Grandma's house, they totally overdid it. I walked out in the morning and saw a brand new mini bike. Not knowing it was for me – and actually suspecting it was for little Henry – I didn't react in any special way which, of course, brought me trouble. Elaine immediately accused me of peeking.

I had been instructed to stay in the hallway until everyone else had gone out to the tree. I didn't really care; I wasn't feeling anything in particular. It had been only a few months since Elaine had whipped me to the point that I had to crawl to my bed and my mind was still numb. Expressionless, I entered the room as they waited for my reaction.

"He must have peeked! No wonder he isn't surprised," she said, as I stood by the edge of the sofa next to the tree. Hank too chimes in, "I told you the box had been opened. You ruined everything!"

I responded, defending myself. "I didn't peek! I didn't know anything about it!"

"Can't even have a surprise," Hank says.

"You little liar!" Elaine states.

I actually wanted to cry, but I didn't. With my spirit sinking even further, I dropped my eyes to the ground. I couldn't stand being accused of something that I hadn't done. Sure, I saw the box behind the door of their bedroom, and I even saw how a little corner had been pulled open, but not by me. So much for a happy day on Christmas.

~.~.~.~

That spring, the events from a few years prior resurfaced: from that August day when demonstrators walked the streets and the air smelled of soot and smoke. Things began to make sense, and now I understood that Martin Luther King had been shot. The black kids in school were somber. The civil rights movement was coming to a head and phrases like "Black Power," "Black Panthers," and "Crips," were prevalent, as was the new attitude of my black classmates.

A few months later, just a couple days before school was to end for the summer, news came in the morning that Senator Robert Kennedy had also been killed. The entire school was let out. When I got home, my aunt was listening to the news when I heard her say, "It better not have been a black man!"

The summer between fourth and fifth grade proved to be as challenging as the school year. Little League was nearly finished and home life was getting nastier by the day, as Elaine would constantly punish me for having a "look" on my face. She would say, "Wipe that smirk off your face, you little bastard."

I didn't know what she was talking about. I didn't have a smirk on my face, at least not intentionally, and how I was supposed to "wipe it off" was incomprehensible anyway.

She would follow up her remarks by jumping up from the couch in a charge and slapping me repeatedly about the face then ordering me to, "Get out of my sight, God damn you!"

This, I was glad to do and I would go to my room or outside, usually in the backyard or garage. Once by myself, I would ponder her actions and wonder what I had to do to prevent them from happening again. It was always the same conclusion: this was a pattern – the same pattern my older sister weathered. That would be the outcome, it seemed, just weathering the many assaults.

Not allowed off the property, I even had to ask permission to go out front. This ate at me because little Henry, who was three years younger, was not required to ask permission and could come and go as he pleased. He could even cross the street and play with the kids in the neighborhood whereas I couldn't.

Despite the unfairness of this treatment, the most hurtful punishment they could give me was taking away my sports. When I was grounded for "having a smirk" or using the wrong tone of voice, Elaine would tell me I could not go to baseball practice or the game. This would be for periods of ten to twenty days. When I would return to practice, the coach would be mad because he thought I was being irresponsible. Fortunately my godfather would speak up and let him know what was going on in my home life. After that the coach seemed to understand and, when I made the games, I played shortstop.

Once, my coach even called Elaine to tell her it was important for me to be there, but Elaine reprimanded him and told him what a terrible kid I was and that she needed to punish me. Fortunately, my godfather again talked to Elaine and asked her to find another way to punish me because she was, in fact, punishing the whole team. My godfather had a certain degree of influence over Elaine and used his appeal to reach out to her. I was fortunate he lived right across the street. He is still an angel in my life.

My godmother would invite Elaine over for coffee and, when she returned, she said I could play baseball again.

With the exception of Sheila, no other neighbors came to Elaine's. It was also very seldom that Elaine was invited to the neighbors'.

Most of the time, she would call and invite herself. I can remember her walking across the street to Sheila's in her nightgown because she was too lazy to get dressed. This really was a disgusting sight. She had a blue nightie that only went halfway down her thighs.

She usually stayed in her nightgown until eleven or so and then, with determination, she would get up and go change. As with everything in her house, it always revolved around her. She would make an announcement, "Well I better get dressed now. I have things to do," then direct Cindy or I to clean up her coffee cup and plate from the toast she had us make for breakfast.

On school days, Cindy and I would come home to a mess. Elaine's robe would be on the couch. Her cup – which was usually half full – and a doughnut box would be on the coffee table. The bathroom would have towels on the floor and dirty laundry left flung about. This would have to be picked up and washed, then folded and put away.

It was gross going into Elaine's underwear drawer to put her panties and bras away. First off, her room was a cluttered mess. The floor was a dumping field full of obstacles that merely found a place to land. The dressers were piled high with clothes and ironing, the drawers crammed and ajar.

Next to the bed on Hank's side was this large chair with shirts piled high off the back. He laid his pants there. If we needed money for milk or bread he would say, "In my pants, there on the chair. Get out what you need."

I didn't like the idea of going in his pants pocket because Elaine had referred to me as a thief so many times I felt they didn't trust me. I was afraid I would be accused of stealing.

I actually began to believe that I might be destined to become a thief. My belief system had been rocked to the point that with everything I did, I made sure I couldn't be accused of stealing.

Hank liked for me to get him coffee also. I didn't really mind getting it for him because he worked hard all the time, and would seldom ask. I would usually just bring him a cup while I was getting Elaine's.

As a rule, Hank always kept busy. Very seldom would he be in front of the television, and definitely not during the day. During the day, if he wasn't at work, he and I would keep busy around the house, usually on a car, or fixing a leak under the house or doing something in the attic. The worst chore, however, was cleaning the garage. He would start out nice and then he would get pissed. I would end up cleaning up everything because Elaine would intervene and say, "Eddie can do that, you just relax dear."

I didn't mind. I had nothing else to do and, besides, if I worked really hard he would let me ride my bike up and down the street for twenty minutes or so when we were done. This was his way of rewarding me for my work and I appreciated the warmth of the privilege.

That wasn't always the case.

I am instructed to remove a 2x4 that is attached to the side of the garage with carriage bolts that have rusted over the years. It is impossible. There is no way. Hank tells me to get the sledgehammer and to bust it off. I try but I am not strong enough to splinter the wood off the bolts.

In a fit of rage, he grabs the long handled sledge from me and begins striking at the wood. Sweat is pouring off his brow as he continues to slam the tool into the wood.

Without warning, the piece breaks free as the bolts, not the wood, snap. Directly into my face goes the 2x4, stunning me for a moment as my eyes tear up.

"PUSSY!" he yells at me. "You're nothing but a PUSSY!"

~.~.~.~

The neighbor's reactions when I was first allowed to cross the street assured me they were keeping an eye on me. Bee was a Native American and married to Frank, an older guy that loved to tinker in his garage. No matter where he was, his tall can of Coors was within reach. With raised eyebrows, she commented to me about little Henry being allowed to go across the street before I was. She wondered if Elaine and Henry were really that dumb to think the neighborhood didn't understand what was going on. It was so very obvious that I was being abused and denied the same privileges that my cousin took for granted.

Frank approached Hank and asked him if it would be okay if on the weekends I helped strip wire for the copper. Granted permission, we spent hours standing out in his backyard with a hook knife in one hand and wire in the other. He showed me how to cut a piece about ten feet long and tie the end to an eyelet he fastened to his gate. Then we would back up until the wire was taut and slice away the edge of the plastic coating. With a smooth stroke I could get a few feet at a time then step up and start my stroke again. In the mean time, he would take a much bigger stroke because of his reach. It wasn't long before we found ourselves racing through boxes of scrap wire he had brought home from work. At the end of the month we would load it all up in the trunk of his car and haul it down to the scrap yard. He would give me five bucks for helping him, which was fine with me. Just being able to hang out at his house was all I wanted, and I'm sure he knew it.

If I could, I would spend hours at his house on the weekends. As soon as I got up in the morning I would race to make sure all my work was done so there would be no reason to be denied. I had a system that included cutting the lawn (along with the rest of the yard work) each Saturday morning. I learned to anticipate what Elaine and Henry might want so I could leave and hang out at Frank's house. It became a habit for Hank to come out in the morning on a Saturday or Sunday stand on the front porch and yell for me. Frank would just look at me with a knowing expression and tell me to hurry up and run along before I got in trouble.

I could detect a bit of jealousy from Hank when he would ask me why I was always over at Frank's. Then he would go on to say, "If you need more to do I'm sure I can find plenty around here for you, you get what I'm getting at?" I would try and avoid responding because I knew what would happen if I did.

"You get what I'm getting at?" If I had a nickel for every time he said that.

Sometimes avoiding the question would work and other times it wouldn't, depending on Hank's mood. When it didn't work, I would get a swift kick or a smack upside the head. If he was really pissed, I would get knocked around pretty good accompanied by a verbal lashing full of insults.

It was one of those things where he liked Frank and respected him, as Frank never gave him a reason not to. Because I was also learning something by being there, Hank was in an unjustifiable position if he denied me going over. That still didn't stop him, but it did help my cause. Sometimes, Hank would just say he needed my help, which was alright because I didn't mind that either. It gave me a chance to try to please him, which is what I really wanted anyway. Again, my belief system had been hijacked by the need to please him and everybody else.

From across the street, Frank called out to Hank to ask if he could borrow me later on this afternoon around one o'clock.

"Sure, that would be fine."

Deep inside, I felt my concealed joy, as I knew what Frank was up to.

I would watch the clock in anticipation and remind Hank that the time was near and that Frank was expecting me to help him with that plumbing leak under his house. "Okay, you better get going," and he would walk out and sit on the porch as I left for the other side of the street.

With a gleam in his eye and that smile on his face, Frank would welcome me and say, "Help me get those pipe wrenches and things from the garage, Eddie," in a voice loud enough for Hank to hear.

As we approached the back steps leading into his home, he would purposely drop a handful of wrenches or other tools, knowing that Hank would understand the noise of a pipe wrench hitting the ground.

Once inside his peaceful home where all was neat and with the curtain pulled closed, we would set the wrenches down. Frank would sit me in his chair and turn on a baseball game as his wife, Bee, would make us lunch.

Two more of my "Angels" seeing me through.

Mr. Treheil, who lived three doors down on my side of the street, always had a smile for me. Whenever I walked by I could smell his cigar and, if he was out front or in his garage, he would wave at me or talk to me and tell me what a great kid I was.

His wife was very quiet and they both kept to themselves, as did most of the neighbors, but they always had that friendly smile for me.

Like a small village, the immediate neighbors had an awareness about them. They knew what was going on and had a subtle way of letting me know they cared. Coming from a generation that was taught to respect the privacy of others and to keep opinions to themselves, minding their own business was only appropriate. Still, they put it out there for me, this energy to harness, empowering me. I understood they were aware of my circumstances and the clarity of separation in our household. There were Elaine's children and then there was us. The two orphan siblings that paid their way.

The Money

As time went on and I got older, my feelings about living at Elaine's began to take on new meaning. I became more aware of the money they received from the state for providing a place for Cindy and me to live. It was natural to begin to wonder how this money played into their role as parents. My reasoning began a sorting process that asked questions like, "Why do these people make us do all the work and why is there little, if any, affection from them?"

Life there was unbalanced in relation to their own children and, if they loved us as their own, it would be equal in most respects. My young mind understood the equation and sum of inadequacy.

It seemed that the money played a big part in our presence in Elaine's home. Sure, at Christmas there were many gifts under the tree that were most fairly distributed in terms of value. This wasn't, however, about physical possessions. This was about warmth that all children craved, a craving Cindy and I lived with. It was about paying our way as we had done since day one. Since the day we arrived from Georgia.

Cindy and I had only each other. We knew that and could depend on that only. Everything else was unstable. Hank and Elaine had won a serious victory in court. They had proven to the entire clan their superiority.

Any support we would get from our other aunts and uncles or grandmother was now gone.

Beaten back by Elaine's aggressive and tenacious style, the rest of the family was now barred from any contact with us. We were severed from them both physically and emotionally, and their names were never to be mentioned again. We had been conditioned. We knew better, as this was a sore subject and a lot of feelings were hurt on both sides. The allegations were hateful and, in Elaine's eyes, Cindy was held to blame for most of it.

As a result of the outcome, it was clear to Elaine and Henry that Cindy did not want to be there. Her testimony clearly outlined the mistreatment of us in the household. Instead of taking the out the court offered, she chose to come back to be with me. This was a brave act considering all the abuse. Elaine would not let her live this down and Cindy had to know that before she made her decision. She gave up her opportunity for freedom because of our pact to always stay together and, as a result, I bore severe guilt knowing she stayed for me.

I felt her pain every time she received a beating. Whenever I heard it coming, I would go to be there with her. I wanted to show her that I was strong and would do whatever I could to protect her, even if it meant simply being with her during her pain. For Cindy, this pain was great and it came from many directions.

As lonely as I was, I always knew that my sister's pain was worse because, on top of the physical and emotional abuse from Elaine and Hank, Cindy also had to endure the loss of the mother she had known for the first few years of her life. Cindy had a taste of the love a child has for her mother.

As for me, I had never known the heartache of detachment except for being separated from my friend Popie and the farm. As for my mother, I had no memory of her. However, Cindy did, and she missed her dearly, always clinging to the hope that someday she would return to be with us.

When the social worker was due to visit, Elaine would brief us and tell us that we had better not make reference to anything that would cause her trouble. It was almost comical the way she would bring us in, sit us down then tell us how, despite the way she treated us, she loved us and was only trying to shape us into something respectable. She warned us that we needed to be very careful because the social worker could take us away and send us to juvenile hall where we would be separated and stuck until we turned eighteen. Of course we knew better and when she would get done prepping us, Cindy and I would leave the room and nod our head to each other affirming that we knew it was all just a bunch of bullshit.

We wondered if going to court had any impact on how the social worker would view Elaine and Hank. Could it be that they were under a microscope or, possibly, that the social worker didn't even know about the custody battle. After the social worker left, Elaine would tell us that we did very well and then send us on our way to do more chores.

I wondered if the social worker ever noticed how nice and clean the house was when she would visit. After all, Cindy and I worked our butts off to get it nice for her visit. I wish she would have asked us what we did as far as helping out around the house. It would have been hilarious to tell her how we washed and cleaned every day while Elaine sat on her butt and filled her ashtray with boogers. That chance never came, though, as we were never asked such questions. The social worker would just take a look at us and Elaine would dismiss us to go "play."

Elaine's concern for the money became clear to me that summer. Panicked that the check was late by a couple of days, she sat me down and told me that she was going to tell the social worker she needed more money or they would have to take us back. She wanted me to know that she really didn't mean it, but that she could get them to come up with more money by threatening them.

This manipulation was typical of her. She didn't seem to think about our feelings or how, as children, we might interpret our security as it hung in the balance of her games. I believed she would push as far as she could go to get her way, never backing down, even if it meant forcefully making her point.

Admiration Or Respect

There's something about turning eleven that makes a boy feel like he has moved up in rank, while losing himself in a place somewhere between being a child and not yet being a teenager. Perhaps it was because I was a year older than everyone else in my class, or maybe because I had grown up differently. Regardless, I felt older, more mature and much wiser than my classmates.

Schoolwork came easy and without challenge. Simple math seemed to be the focus of our daily lessons and the rest was just reading chapters, with a quiz at the end of the week, and never any homework.

Each Wednesday, the ESL bus parked in front of the school and half the class was excused to be tutored in English. The rest of us would have free time to catch up on reading or to practice playing paper football at our desk with a person sitting nearby as the afternoon passed. When the school bell rang we bolted for the hallway and raced to the exit of the old beige two-story. Crowding in the single opening, we filed out onto the street, usually to gather at the nearest corner to see who would fight, then proceed to the park to get it on.

Last year school ended on the day that Bobby Kennedy was shot. A few months before, the country lost Martin Luther King and, shortly thereafter, the Civil Rights Act was signed into law. A stark difference in attitudes seemed to be present among the black kids of the 'hood as this school year began.

There was an air about them, a sense of empowerment and identity that I had not seen before; a reflection of confidence and unity. Even as a fifth grader, I could clearly see change had made its way to the old elementary school on the corner of Civic Center and Raitt. Afros were in and the stylish looks were accompanied by clothing defining heritage and pride. In the hip pockets of the dark colored jeans with tall cuffs I could see the handle of a pick comb protruding, many of which were made of metal and some with wooden handles that could be gripped and, on occasion, used as weapons.

The Jackson Five, Motown's hot discovery, was taking off and, on Saturdays, Fat Albert made us laugh as he zipped through his neighborhood on an undersized skateboard. He, too, had an afro and a smile that melted viewers, including me. What I saw was a character that portrayed real life in a neighborhood not so different than my own. It was a sneak peek at black culture in the suburbs, with characters just like the ones that attended my school, but in cartoon form with story lines just as familiar. How amazing were the lessons we learned in front of the television without even knowing it.

Fifth grade also brought with it a new level of violence. We graduated from using our fists to using our belts. An instant equalizer equipped with a brass buckle that hooked over and into the strap, accommodating a quick release. Wrapped around your hand a few times it extended your reach a good twelve inches and your foe certainly didn't want to get caught by the buckle. Troopers used this as their weapon of choice when gang fights broke out. Witnessing them beating each other with it shaped the complexion of our neighborhood and added to the viciousness when tension flared.

One afternoon as school let out, my Chicano friend Pete was squaring off against a black kid named Ricky, who was much taller and bigger. Pete was short, like me, and on the small side. Today, we took it to the corner of Ninth and Raitt in the parking lot near the handball courts, where they began to throw blows. This was a good fight: both Ricky and Pete had been there before. Once winded, Ricky pulled his belt off and used it as a strap, folding in half and swinging it over his head, reminiscent of the way Hank and Elaine would beat Cindy and I.

The lesson of the day came when Pete smoothly pulled his belt off and wrapped it about his hand. He stepped in and caught Ricky twice with the buckle sending him like a beaten dog running down the street. I learned a lot that afternoon, including the benefits of an equalizer in a street fight.

Many of my friends were approaching the point in their young life where individual identity begins to take hold and shape your image for others to see. I was no exception. The life I knew, life at home, had shaped me uniquely, including the attitude I carried with me on the street. Although we lived on the edge of a very rough neighborhood, the fact that we lived there was enough to grant passage to and from school. Though not always without incident, I still had the right of passage being from the 'hood.' Again, I was content having the escape of school as my sanctuary away from Elaine and Hank.

My identity also included a need to dominate, which surfaced on the playground in a competitive manner. Different from home life, this was my self expression, an unbridled release of emotions that had been bottled up deep inside. It gave me clout with the others from my 'hood, along with the recognition I couldn't get at home.

As it turned out, Elaine studied nursing and started working the three-to-eleven shifts at night. Hank was away on long hauls giving me wide open afternoons all to myself. I found my routine playing basketball at the park, tinkering with the mini bikes, or building my ten-speed bicycle from random parts. Still I maintained an independent persona on the streets and was accepted by most.

At home, it was always the same. Roberta now had the task of cooking and would make dinner that consisted of Hamburger Helper. Sometimes she would get creative with a Spanish dish that she had learned at school. Other than cooking, she did nothing, leaving Cindy to clean the entire house and do everyone's laundry. She and I would fold the laundry together in the evenings while Roberta sat and watched television with her little brother.

When Elaine would leave, she put Roberta in charge. This seemed strange since Cindy was the same age. Then again, if you look at our role in the house, we were little more than servants – caretakers who maintained the menial duties of the household and represented a paycheck from the county for the roof provided over our heads.

Spitefully, I rebelled against Roberta's authority, remembering days when I was younger. She could push me around then but now I wouldn't take it. The day of reckoning eventually came, one weekend when Elaine left taking Cindy with her. I was there with Roberta and little Henry alone. In her bossy manner, she began yelling and threatening like she had done in the past so many times, insisting I do something for her. I refused. In the same fashion as Elaine, she came charging at me, attempting to slap my face, however, this time I was waiting with something special.

I knew better and, with confidence I defied her, knowing I could handle her. As she slapped at me, I came over the top with a right and tagged her on top of her head. This was the first time I ever hit back. I just wasn't going to take it from her.

She freaked! She screamed like she was dying, crying out as she stepped back in amazement. Her eyes were welling up with tears, a look of shock taking over as she realized the days of hitting me were over. Standing her distance, she screamed that she was going to tell Elaine and that I was in for it. I already knew that anyway, so it didn't matter. What mattered was that I had made my point and things were going to change.

When Elaine came home, it was only seconds before Roberta ran to her and snitched. Elaine came charging at me while I was on the back porch sweeping the floor. She started slapping me about the head repeatedly, telling me that I better never raise a hand to Roberta again.

All the while, I knew I had won. She could pound on me until she was blue in the face – which she did – and it wouldn't change a thing.

That was the last time Roberta ever tried to slap me. I was only eleven, and she was sixteen, but I had experienced enough anger and brutality already and was not going to tolerate anymore from her. Even though she did not like me for that, she did show me respect from then on whenever she said something. She began speaking to me politely and she learned how to talk to me in a manner that was not threatening.

This was a major turning point in our relationship and, even though she didn't do her fair share, she began to treat Cindy and me with more respect.

~.~.~.~

Later that spring, baseball started up and I began my first year of the Majors. I was drafted to the Astros, where my coach was a young guy about eighteen years old. His little brother, Robert, was on the team. I played right field, typical for a first year player. I made the best of it, especially as a batter. Because I was small, it was hard to pitch and most of the time I would draw a walk. Most important to me was the concept of belonging to a team. Avoiding seeing Elaine because of her work schedule, I also avoided trouble, which included being put on restriction. Unlike prior years when I would lose the privilege for having a "look on my face," this was the first year I didn't miss any games.

After baseball finished, I found myself spending more time just cruising around. Low rider Stingrays were in so I collected old bicycle forks, cut them with a hacksaw and pounded them into shape to extend my front wheel out as far as possible. This made it easy to pop wheelies and ride for yards without the front wheel touching the ground.

Elaine continued to work the three-to-eleven shifts, sleeping till noon. This gave me the opportunity to get my work done in the morning and time it so I wasn't there when she woke up. With all the yard work and my part of the cleaning done (and her nursing shoes polished) I was out the door by late morning. Avoiding Elaine was paramount in my life. Learning the value of staying out of her sight helped me understand the dynamics of my place in her house and how I could better my life by obscurity. As a younger child she had said to me many times, "Get out of my sight," and now I had it down pat.

For a quarter we could go to the plunge at SAC, short for Santa Ana College. I would take little Henry with me and then ditch him once we were there. He wasn't allowed in the deep end because of his age, so I didn't have to hang with him. By the time we would get back, Elaine would be getting dressed for work. I could go the whole day without crossing her path which, in and of itself, kept me out of trouble. After she left for work I would go down the street to my friend Butch's house and hang out, lift weights or just rap. His parents were always nice to me but they didn't like little Henry, probably because he was spoiled, which was really no fault of his own.

This was a byproduct of our household. The neighbors did not approve of my treatment or that of Cindy. As a rule, they said little to Elaine and Henry, if anything at all. For me, they were always outgoing and reassuring. As for little Henry, they tolerated him and sometimes, even though it wasn't his fault, they stood off or commented about how spoiled he was: a direct result of the disapproval they felt toward Elaine and Hank. I realized this to be true for Roberta also and I felt sorry for her as she was also a product (and poor result) of being raised by a woman with bad parenting skills.

I gained reassurance from this. There was satisfaction in knowing that, despite my treatment at home, the people in the neighborhood knew what was going on and were not impressed by Elaine's rearing of her real children. My sister and I were special to everyone and, sometimes, this is all that got us through. In a way, it was like we were in a small village and it was known by all what was going on. They were our support group, even if it meant something as simple as an approving nod from across the street.

~.~.~.~

The dominant traits that were maturing in me were taking me down a dangerous course. No longer the shy little child that arrived in Santa Ana years back, I was now looking to prove my worth by overrunning rivals including other kids on my street. Despite my size, I was confident and unable to control my rage driven assaults on the kids who crossed me.

Carefully, I balanced my actions so the adults on my street still admired me but many kids, especially those away from immediate view, were well aware and seldom dared to incite me. I knew the value of image by now, having learned it on the street and at the park. Keeping this side of me a secret was important for maintaining my image with the adults who gave me approval and support.

I had now earned the respect, or perhaps fear, of the kids in the 'hood' and it empowered me as one who could handle himself in the streets. But I was becoming a bully of another sort. I was now strapped with the need to feed and validate this behavior.

The downside of this was that I had learned how to manipulate, through force, to get what I wanted. I learned how to overrun the obstacles, rather than negotiate with finesse. I would power through my opponents, leaving them no choice once backed into a corner but to fight or back down. Initially, I established respect from my peers. It would be several years before I would realize that there was a better approach.

Why I did this or had this trait was beyond me at the time. I don't know if it was a learned behavior or inherited, but it has always been with me. Later in life, this would be explained – and it's amazing how the treatment of a child can affect the overall personality of them as an individual. Was this the lack of nurturing as a baby, or the impact of being abandoned as an infant? I do miss that nurturing. I can only reflect back to that now, but it's such an important part of identifying love.

If you do not know love as a child, then how do you learn to love? Love is definitely taught and learned. Some could argue that it's instinctive, as I believe it *is* instinctual for a parent to love a child, however, I know it is *not* an instinct for a child to love their caretakers. I wanted recognition from

Elaine and Hank, and I did think I loved them, as I thought I owed them that. I know now that I really didn't love them any more than they loved me; a fact that would become apparent later in my life.

Compassion For The Coward

It was with this attitude that I entered the sixth grade. Confidence dripped off me as I walked onto the schoolyard and was greeted by others who were also caught up in this pre-pubescent state. That behavior that is only cool when your twelve and when your trying to be worthy of the onrushing teenage years.

My teacher, Mr. Seplack, was creative and had a way of turning our smartass remarks into humor. I enjoyed his class as it was based more around mechanics and science. He did things like explain how a light bulb worked and how an electrical current could be generated. For me, this put my brain in gear and helped me leave my attitude at the door.

Three of us, Brett, Calvin and myself, were selected to visit Santiago, a school on the north side that the rich kids went to. We were in a three-way-tie with the best scores in the school so we represented Fremont in a one day fieldtrip.

And what a trip it was.

We were all trippin' when we saw what these kids were into. Suddenly, I was aware of school in a whole different light. First off, there were no students of color. There were only white kids there and they were all dressed like they were going to church. The classroom was full of creative ideas and the students were assembling globes out of paper Mache. At Fremont, we were competing to see who could take apart a lawnmower engine and put it back together the fastest. I won that competition. I'm sure all the years working on cars had something to do with that. Bottom line was Santiago was pumping out intelligence and Fremont was pumping out trouble.

It was during that year that I found my first job. Early evenings I would get picked up by a van with several other kids inside, most were black and a few years older. They messed with me a little, really only teasing me and calling me "the cracker" as we drove to other cities, selling subscriptions for the Orange County Register. At the end of the evening I would have more orders than most, but I was always second to Jeffrey. I never knew how he did it but he always got more.

I saved my money and talked my Grandma Hansen into using her charge card at Montgomery Wards to buy me a mini bike that had a four horsepower engine. I paid her back every cent with the money I earned from that job. Little Henry inherited the mini bike they had given me the Christmas before.

One Saturday afternoon, Hank took Little Henry and I and our mini bikes to a dirt lot behind the old Consumer City. As we were riding around in the small mounds of dirt, two other boys joined us with their new AT70's. These bikes were the "kind" and it was fun to watch them fly by us.

Hank was on his old Honda 150, keeping tabs on us as he viewed us from the top of a hill.

For some unknown reason, Hank got riled up and rode over to the boys, signaling them to stop. Little Henry and I rode up to them and then, without cause, he said to the Mexican boys, "I have a knife too." I was immediately embarrassed by his actions.

The boys looked stunned by his statement as they hurried off. It wasn't long before the boy's father showed up and signaled Hank to come on over to him.

I sat amazed as I watched this man walk up to Hank and begin to hit him over the top of his head with a fist. Then he would ask Hank a question and Hank would shrug his shoulders. Again he would hit him over the top of his head, step back and ask him a question.

Clearly, Hank was a coward. He could say an inappropriate comment to this man's young teenage boys, but he was not man enough to talk back to their father.

I watched in shame. When it was over, Hank came back, riding up like nothing happened and said we had to go. As we loaded up the bikes he says to me, "He is just a bigger man then I am," implying he was too big to fight back.

Today, I learned compassion.

~.~.~.~

At home that afternoon the feeling of shame continued to linger from the events earlier in the day. Something had happened and I was being yelled at by Elaine, then Hank got up and started punching me. I just covered up and found that place I would go to. It's a strange feeling to stand still while a coward beats on you.

My fear of him left me that day as I watched him sit there like an idiot and get hit repeatedly. Unlike me, he had a choice and could have left and, unlike me, he had the power to fight back but he didn't. Unlike me, Hank was a coward.

Again, I started having thoughts about the gun in the top drawer. I didn't care if I lived or died, and I thought if I killed myself they would have to answer questions about the scars on my body. As I walked by the drawer, I felt this energy begin to fill my chest and back. My spiritual visitor had come to me, entering my body and telling me no, that this was not the way. As I left their bedroom and walked down the hall toward my room, I realized those thoughts of ending it all were nothing but a shortcut to solving my challenges. What would come of it anyway?

Although I knew I had no control over my thoughts, I vowed to myself never to seriously consider this again.

Educated On Civic Center And Raitt

My attitude was changing as rapidly as the boundary of my turf, I found myself callused with the struggles at home and the racial tensions of the street. Ninth Street, where I lived, was one of the less violent streets in the 'hood. Although it was not gang infested, it was controlled, and occasionally we would get a splash of the life just a few blocks south. Civic Center Drive as it is now called – formally known as Eighth Street – was a clear separation of the neighborhoods in this quadrant of Santa Ana. Raitt Street ran north and south about 500 feet west of my aunt's house and we backed up to the families on Eighth. It was nothing unusual for the police to come through our backyard looking for someone that hopped the fence, fleeing from them.

I wasn't sure where I was headed, except that I was going there on *my* terms as far as the street went. At home, it was a different story. I learned to play the part of the servant as much as possible. Cindy and I, now settled back in after the custody battle a few years earlier, had our routine. With Hank on the road and Elaine working three-to-eleven shifts as a nurse at a nearby hospital, I finessed my day accordingly. She was at work when I got home from school and I made sure I was asleep when she got home from work. I learned the value of timing and usually managed to stay out of her sight.

Hank suffered a heart attack a couple years earlier and had recovered. He still worked long hours. He used to carry little white pills to help him keep awake while he drove trucks, and now he carried nitroglycerin for chest pains. He was hardly ever home during the week but made it home for most of the weekends. As I grew older, my relationship with him changed. Like the old lion standing ground against the youngsters as they aged, even at twelve, it was apparent that I threatened his dominance.

Tension on the street was growing daily. Blacks, or *niggers* as Elaine called them, were a strong sect in the city south of Eighth and west of Raitt. Fremont, my school, was on this corner. At school, the blacks ran in groups: not really *gangs* but groups of ten or twelve. If you walked by, you were almost sure to get a comment but, in all fairness, it went with the turf.

Regardless of what your color was, you had an attitude. Several years earlier, the 'hood was filled with fear from the spillover to our city from the Watts Riots. Santa Ana had one of the largest populations of black families and they were united in their quest for equal rights as much here as anywhere. During the riots, the police had to blockade Ninth and Raitt in an attempt to herd civil rights marchers toward El Salvador Park for containment.

Hank was out on his porch with his gun and so were a few of the neighbors. We were all expecting the emerging crowd to flow toward us as we listened to the radio for the vague details. The police showed up in force with several cars speeding down our street toward Raitt, heading the rioters off and moving them west. Along the way, rioters set buildings on fire and many shots were heard. Consumer City was hit hard and the Santa Ana Lumber yard near Fifth and Raitt went up in flames. It seemed to burn forever.

This, however, was a few years past and the color dial of the city was swinging to shades of brown. Third-generation Mexican families were having babies and the same gangs that had formed years before became organized and established their own street boundaries. There was East Side, Cross Warner, Delhi, Santa Anita, Shades of Brown, and then there was Fx-Troop. FxTroop centralized in and controlled El Salvador Park. From there, it moved south, bordering the riverbed and trickling into areas that, at one time, were completely black.

Now dwindling in numbers, blacks organized with many of the young teens claiming the "Crips," wearing jackets with the fur lined collars. Elaine and Hank bought me a similar jacket and, believe me, it didn't go over well walking through the streets with it on. I couldn't explain this to my aunt or uncle as they did not have a clue as to the dangers these gangs represented.

Low riders lined up at El Salvador and dozens of gang bangers hung out. Tenth Street bordered the north side of the park and was preferred, as it had all the shade from the large willow trees that lined the angled parking spots.

El Salvador Park was in complete control of FxTroop, making it a place to avoid. For the most part, you didn't go into the park after dark and, when troopers were out, you weren't.

FxTroop was one of the first organized gangs in the city. They literally controlled the Westside between McFadden and Washington, and from Fairview to Flower. This gang had started with older brothers from prior generations and was now heading for its heyday just a few years away.

Baseball was different as well. Many of the kids dropped out as the street called for them. Still, I was competitive and loved to play. Our team, the Astro's, sucked. I played a lot of positions and finally settled in at first base. Second base was Eddie O, a kid from Second Street. We hung out some, but not a lot, mainly at school and before or after the games as team-mates do. A few years from now he would become a vicious example of racism and what the gangland lifestyle of our turf could breed. It was an amazing enlightenment for a kid growing up on the rough side of town, learning about the disadvantage of being a minority "white patty" in a neighborhood of color.

There seemed to be daily lessons about racism. For anyone who didn't experience the weaker position of race it may be hard to understand. For me, I learned that racism had little to do with the color of one's skin and mostly to do with the power of numbers. You were either black or brown at the park and, if you were white, you were a minority anywhere south of Ninth and west of Bristol.

Mondo's Market, on the corner of Civic Center and Raitt backed up to El Salvador and drew a lot of business off the kids from the park. Mondo was on top of anyone in his store. If he didn't like you he caught you at the door and everything stopped until you left, which meant anyone that was in the store knew you weren't welcome. Outside on the steps of his store, I learned about numbers and the power that came with it.

It was Easter break and I had just left the park, headed east on Eighth, walking next to Mondo's market on the sidewalk. The mid morning sun had been baking the side of the brick wall and I could feel the radiant heat warm me. Something about trouble: it seems to broadcast a warning signal before you see it. I felt it brewing, that gut feeling in the core of my body, alerting me to canvas the street ahead. From around the corner it unrolled. Three black kids I didn't know came by, riding on Stingrays and, as they approached, the first kid spit in my face. They didn't stop but instead turned and we stared at each other. He turned back around and they kept going.

I wiped the slime off the bridge of my nose and out of my left eye. Rage consumed me as I climbed the steps leading into Mondo's. This was the first time I felt rage on the street. Angry about what had just happened and the wet spot on my t-shirt where I used it to wipe the spit from my face, the feeling in my core continued to grow as I realized this wasn't over. Approaching the counter, I could see through the tinted green glass door several black kids gathering near the bottom of the steps. They were waiting for me.

Again, that intuitive ability alerted me to a dangerous presence. Like so many times before, I knew I would have to fight my way out but, today would be the first time I would have to fight my way out of the *corner market.* Today would also be the first time I was energized by so much rage. The disrespect of this disgusting offense ignited something within that I had never felt before.

Exiting the doors, I tossed the small bag to the side. On the second step we bumped chests like wild goats testing our strength. Exchanging blows, I'm outnumbered. He was quick and taller. I was a blaze of overhands, non-stop taking his ground and backing him down. We were off the steps, onto the sidewalk and heading toward the street and, as I stepped in again, I had to pull back. With brakes screeching, a car swerves to miss him. I stepped back and we looked at each other, and that was it.

The look on his face is of embarrassment and he acknowledges me with a bit of surprise as I picked up my bag and walked on. The kids with him were talking smack but he wasn't talking at all. He knew he had the upper hand with his "boyz," but he also knew he wasn't shit without backup.

That was the first time I really wanted to fuck somebody up. It was the disrespect that pulled this anger from my core. The street was my sanctuary, my freedom, my escape...*call it the fight in the dog*. Outnumbered, it wasn't about the size, it was about *me*, and I wouldn't let anyone take that from me.

All the way home, I remembered how I stepped off him because he was headed for the street and I didn't want him to get hit. I also struggled with regret of not stepping into him again, and realized I could have fucked him up by pushing him into the traffic. I realized that element of the street meant I could have beaten him into the car and ended his little dream of dominance. Instead, I stepped off him and left him with the respect from his "boyz" intact. The one thing he knew was that I didn't back down and I wasn't afraid of his numbers. In my mind, there wasn't anyone that could beat me worse than what I got at home.

Again, I realized that I was changing, becoming the product of my home life unleashed unto the streets. The chip on my shoulder continued to grow and a need to prove myself festered. My peers would feed me the attention I craved by engaging me with fist fights or belt buckles, transitioning me into an adolescent just looking to unleash. Inside, I felt like an island, alone in so many ways. I was independent of the others who ran the streets, yet was associated by my mere presence in the 'hood,' and I always held myself on guard with a stance of defiance and a demand for respect.

Would I ever dare to run or back down? There was no need to even ask this question, for the streets were my refuge, the balance of my life. I was learning about family by watching others. My identity became "the little white boy with an attitude."

That attitude was *survival*. I had found a state of mind that cleansed me of the brutality of my aunt's presence, my uncle's cowardly attacks on my eighty-pound body and I had determined not to allow this to happen any-where else in my realm. I feel anger, resentment and even hatred as it begins to form, as my heart continues to rebuke my situation, identifying love from one stranger and ignorance from another. Trying to understand.

Departure

One Saturday night in late May, after dinner, I find myself washing the dishes. Cindy was out with Roberta on a double date. Standing on the red and white metal chair at the sink, I could see the moon's illumination through the wood-framed window. The tree limbs next door looked like giant arms reaching into the sky, swaying in the moonlight.

I was just finishing up when Elaine came into the kitchen and began to speak, "I have a phone number that supposedly belongs to your mother." She then tells me to dry my hands off and to be ready to talk to her if she gets her on the line. This was bizarre. I had never received as much as a birthday card from my real mother and now Elaine was going to put me on the phone line with her.

Elaine dialed the number and said, "Dotty, this is Elaine, your sister Elaine. Here, I have somebody who wants to speak to you," and, just like that, Elaine hands me the phone.

I said, "Hello?"

All I hear is a lady's voice on the other end saying, "Oh my God," while breaking into tears, crying. The line went dead.

This was heavy and I wondered if that would be all I would ever know of the woman who was my mother.

Elaine didn't wait more than a few seconds before saying, "Back to the dishes! And don't forget to sweep the floor when you're done. Oh, by the way, Roberta broiled some steak, so you need to clean that and change the foil."

The foil was my idea, seeing as I was the one that would have to clean the stove. I would leave it covered with foil after each cleaning so it would be easier to clean after she used it.

Elaine seemed to have no concept of my feelings. She was so "matter of fact." I'm twelve years old and have just heard what is supposed to be my mother's voice for the first time in my life. She simply dismisses me from the phone and orders me back to the dishes.

The next day, Elaine called her again but, this time, I would not be allowed to speak to her even though I wanted to. Elaine said, "You don't need to, you already did."

This didn't surprise me, after all: I knew better by now. Elaine, as always, was in control and this time wouldn't be any different. Cindy did get to talk to her, which was great for her. She was ecstatic! Her mom was coming to get her. She was going to be rescued, finally, after all these years.

Cindy thought she and I would be rescued and we would live

happily ever after. That was Cindy, I loved my sister, but she had different ideas than I. Maybe it was because she actually spent time living with her mother, that she had a chance to bond and connect with her. I didn't. I resented her for that. Not Cindy, my mother. I didn't know why she left me and I didn't understand how a mother could do that to her child.

Hank and Elaine never let me forget that my father was a racketeer, a professional thief, and a loan shark. They usually reminded me by saying how I would be just like him; that there was a flaw in the genes and I would be contaminated for life.

They were right in some respects. In some ways, I *was* like my father. Things came naturally to me and I easily understood how things worked. I understood that Elaine and Henry were fucked up and that their kids were fucked up because of them. After all, if my father's traits could predetermine what I would be, Little Henry and Roberta were really headed for a life. Again, my bitterness was surfacing in the world that surrounded me. Truly, I wish I had more empathy for them, after all, they too were victims of their own parents' behaviors.

My mother called back a few more times over the next couple of weeks. Again, I was not allowed to talk to her but I didn't think a lot about it. Cindy was really into it and she couldn't wait. They planned to be here in early July, that's all I knew, and I continued on with very little expectation.

Three years earlier, I had weathered a custody battle and my gut warned me that incident would pale in comparison to what was to come. As the days passed and the first of July approached, Cindy told me that our mother would be here soon. She tried to prepare me to expect to leave but somehow I didn't think it would go down that way.

My spiritual visitor has been so close these last few weeks. I spend much time alone wondering about the unknown events that will soon unfold before me. Deep inside, I know I will not be leaving, because I was never part of the equation to begin with. This is about my sister. Cindy will be 18 years old soon, the money will stop and she will be leaving me. I am scared for her.

At night I don't sleep, but instead lay in my bed, pondering thoughts of being alone. This is the first time I will ever know life without Cindy. Why do I know my mother is coming for Cindy? It is as though I realize that, many years ago, a deal must have been struck. Elaine would take us kids, but our mother would stay out of the picture. Why else would the timing, out of nowhere work, out this way?

~.~.~.~

It's the fourth of July and I'm twelve years old. Cindy and I have been waiting for this day for a long time. The morning sun shines bright in the eastern sky as it burns through the side windows over the kitchen sink. I was standing in this exact spot six weeks ago doing the dishes, hands red from scalding sink water. That was the night Cindy was out and the clean-up chores fell to me – the same night my aunt called me over to the ironing board where the phone was set with the cord stretched taut.

"There's somebody that wants to talk to you," she had said callously, handing me the phone. That was the night that I first heard my mothers voice as she broke down into tears and hung up. All I've heard since is that she is coming.

They are due to arrive sometime this morning. Elaine is actually up and dressed and it's not even nine o'clock. She is making Cindy and I clean and polish everything before our mother gets here with her new husband. Cindy says our mother is stopping in Las Vegas to get married on the way. I guess she is some movie star or has something to do with theater. I remember when I was younger Elaine told me she was a stripper, whatever that is. I was too young and had no idea.

It's almost eleven now and the phone rings. I think it might be her by the way Elaine is talking, so nice and pleasant. When she hangs up the phone she tells me I need to run to the store to get some more milk for the coffee for when they arrive. I mention that we have almost a half a gallon, but she gives me that cross look and tells me to walk, don't take your bike. I know she has timed this on purpose because she doesn't want me to be there when my mother arrives.

As always, I fly off the steps and tear down the street. This time, I don't jump the hedge along the way as the neighbor doesn't like it. Past the houses leading up to my sacred trees I run, slowing – like I always do – to walk below the giant canopies. Once I am to the other side I again take off to get to the store at full speed.

Pushing open the swinging glass door, I come out of the store and onto the steps that lead down to the sidewalk, the same steps where, a month before, I fought the black kid who spat in my face. I notice a beautiful white Pontiac Bonneville. It looks so out of place for our 'hood. This ride is sweet with a black landau roof and a freshly polished shine. Immediately, I notice the red headed woman in the front seat and the man driving, his hair jet black and styled back with hair spray, and I realize my mother has just passed by me.

A strange sense overtakes me as my excitement dissipates, watching this beautiful car roll down Raitt Street. I have, for the first time in my life

that I can remember, seen my mother and, instead of excitement, I feel flat

and without emotion. I am overcome with anticipation that the letdown I have

just felt is only the beginning.

Instead of running back to the house, I walk, slowly – almost purposely taking my time as, again, I realize that the arrival of my mother will mean the departure of my sister. It only makes sense to me. Cindy will turn eighteen in exactly two weeks. They have come to take her away as she will no longer be allowed to live at the Whitsett's.

About midway in the block from the corner to my aunt's house are the trees that have, for so long, felt spiritual to me. I approach them holding the brown sack containing the creamer and I stop underneath. It is as if the canopy is a blanket of truth for me. I can trust my feeling and I know my sister shall soon be gone. My gaze falls from the shaded limbs to the sidewalk and then to the house as I come closer, noticing the orange tree out front that I have spent countless hours climbing.

I think of the times Cindy and I used to climb it when we were younger. She could always climb higher than I. She loved to spend time in the trees and, as I think, my mind drifts even further back to the days we were in Georgia. I remember the big oak tree with the tire swing, the one that Cindy used to climb in the afternoons and talk to her *Daddy-God* when she was a child as I sat in the dirt nearby and watched her. Again, I realize that in no time at all, my sister will be far away from me, much farther than the top of that tree in Georgia.

Walking up the front steps I gather myself to hide the fear I feel inside, thinking about how I will not have my sister close to me anymore. I don't want to show my emotions, the ones I always manage to keep to myself, my only *true* possessions. I can hear voices from inside the darkened house. There, on the velvet blue sectional, Elaine sits with my mother and her husband. I walk in and Elaine introduces me, "This is Eddie." My mother still sits, she does not get up, and there are no embraces. Cindy is getting coffee ready for them. The awkward moment only lasts long enough for Elaine to order me into the kitchen with the milk. As I return with Cindy and the coffee, I am told I can go outside as she has to talk to my mother. Cindy stays for awhile after I leave.

This is so orchestrated, I think, so planned out. I don't understand why I would be ordered to leave the room. Regardless, I do as I am told and go back to my room. As the day goes on, Cindy and my mother spend time together but I am kept away. Clearly Cindy will be leaving soon and I will be left behind. The connection still numb, I begin to set my mind to the inevitable: I don't like these people.

That evening, I am sent to bed earlier than normal. I understand my mother will be spending the night but they have stepped out and will be back in a while. My mother peeks her head in to tell me she would be back soon. I lay in bed at the end of the long hallway. My mind races with thoughts of life without my sister. Awareness of the day's events linger like the smoke in the air from tonight's Independence Day celebration.

It is much later when I hear them return and get ready to sleep in the front room. Johnny Carson has just ended and Elaine goes to bed. Hank is on the road tonight and will not be home.

Waking in the wee hours of the morning, I hear someone walking down the hall. It's only a few steps from the dining room to the bath, yet there are too many steps for that, so who is it and where are they going?

The steps end just a bit farther down the hall, near Cindy's door, and I can hear movement that isn't familiar to me. Something is going on but I stay still and listen. Soon, I hear a voice, but it is muffled, then more steps leaving the room quickly. Someone had entered my sister's room. My heart races, wondering what to do as I am frozen stiff and cannot move. I listen closely but hear nothing more.

The next morning, my mother and John are up and gone early. They are not spending the night again as Hank is home and angry about something that is kept quiet. I think it had to do with what happened last night.

The days that follow are filled with a wicked energy. I can't pinpoint it but it's about deceit and arrangements and deals made in the past. I am not fooled, only afraid.

~.~.~.~

It has now been two weeks since I "met" my mother. I haven't seen her since the night she peeked her head in and said she would be right back. Today is Cindy's birthday and, surely, this will be it, I think. By mid morning, Elaine is beckoning for her coffee as she always does. Lying in her bed calling out in a pathetic limp voice, "Coffee, coffee," we scramble to get the cream and two spoons of sugar into it. Cindy hands it to me and I take it in. Again, Hank is getting ready to go on the road, somewhere, far away from here.

The ironing board is full of clothes that have been washed and Cindy stands behind it with the iron in her hand. For years, she has ironed for six people, but the pile remains a never ending mound continuously growing, as no one else ever helped her.

As Elaine enters the room with her weekend garb on, I can sense there will be trouble. Today will be a bad day. The sun is again shinning through the kitchen widows as it did just a few weeks ago, the day our mother arrived. The house has not been picked up as of yet and Elaine is already riding Cindy as she sits her carcass on the blue velvet sofa and orders more coffee. There is something intentional in her voice as she begins to provoke my sister. I watch on as Cindy ignores her remarks only to be ridiculed for not responding. I hated the way Elaine would do that. She would set you up with a demeaning remark that, if answered, would be defiance. If we didn't answer then we were being defiant also. There was no way to win, and it was only a matter of time before she would fly off the couch and start beating us.

This woman was sick.

Today would be different though. As soon as Cindy ignored her cruel remarks, she was up and swinging, grabbing her by the hair and beating on her with all of her force. This would be the last time she would beaten Cindy as she dragged her to the door and threw her into the screen then out onto the sidewalk. "You're eighteen years old, get the hell out!" she said as Cindy hit the sidewalk and left. I didn't get to say goodbye, as it happed so quickly.

She was gone. I only heard,

"I Love You, Eddie."

Part III

The theater of that morning's event played over in my mind as I realized that Elaine had planned the final act well before it happened. But of course, Cindy is eighteen today and there will be no more money from the state.

Doing Time

Weeks have gone by and I have not heard from my sister or my mother, and I don't even know if they're nearby. Maybe they're at Grandma Hansen's, I wonder.

Life at the Whitsett's hasn't missed a beat since that day. I'm now in charge of cleaning the entire house. Roberta is never there and little Henry is always out playing. I have been confined to the house, waiting for Jr. High School to finally start, perfecting the creases as I iron. Adjustment is difficult for me. The emotions want to escape from my soul, but for what? Who will care? There is no one to hear. To myself they will be kept, waiting for another day.

School has been in session for almost a week and today's my

birthday. As I'm leaving campus the neighbor girl, Kimmy, calls out and catches up to me. She says she has a surprise for me. We walk and I wonder what's going on as Kimmy and I were really never close enough to share surprises. She wasn't allowed to be too friendly with me because of what went on at our house. She tells me it will only be a minute when I look up and I see my sister. Cindy is running down the street toward me and I'm so happy to see her. I run to her and we grab hold and hang on for the longest time.

Cindy walks with me as we go toward an apartment that she lives in near the school with her mother and John. As we walk she explains to me that there was an arrangement with our mother and Elaine. She also tells me that my mother and John have issues and she doesn't think she will be with them long. "Things happen, Eddie. This will not be a good place for you." She explains that they have no money and they can hardly pay for groceries. Their plans are to leave for Chicago in a few weeks and they want me to go with them. I tell Cindy I don't want to go with them as I feel they're strange to me. I only saw my mother for a few brief moments and she hasn't been back to see me. I have no connection. We say our goodbyes and she tells me she loves me. At the time, I didn't realize I wouldn't see her again for nearly five years.

The weekend comes and I'm called into Elaine's bedroom. She shuts the door and Hank begins to speak as Elaine crawls back into bed.

They explain to me that my mother wants me to go with her and that if I want to I can. Hank is sincere as he states I'm welcome to stay if I would like to. He tells me that he knows what goes on isn't always right but he cares for me and if I stay he will tell her.

This was one of the few "fair" moments I ever remember under their roof. I feel his attempt to reconcile, his words are true and real. Yes, he is right I think, things have never been right here. Then I reply:

"I have already given thought to this. My education is important to me. I want to be an attorney and I want to go to school. If I leave I don't know what will happen, but at least here I know what to expect."

The look in their eyes tells me they understand my double edged remarks and will talk to my mother when she comes over later that night. I wonder if they can begin to grasp even for a moment, the depth of my insight, my ability to know. Like a solder moved up in rank, I have assumed all the responsibilities of my sister. I'm a good soldier, I turn and walk away.

The house has been under construction now for a few weeks and I'm sleeping out in the dining room on the floor as their car pulls up. I hear the doors open and they come up the walk. Hank is agitated already but when he sees my uncle Donald he jumps off the couch and confronts him on the porch. "What the hell are you doing here?!" he demands. They have words and Donald cowers down immediately. He is forced to stay outside but he stays near the porch just in case.

My mother starts in: she has a foul mouth and is confrontational as Elaine tells her I do not want to go with them. They argue and my mother demands to hear it from me, but I lie still and listen as she does not know I'm only a few feet away on the floor behind a dresser. Silently, I observe with only my ears. The words exchanged transcend to a visual, as though I can see through my ears. Inside, my chest is heavy, not with fear but disappointment. Although my mother pleads for me, I know it is merely role playing, an insincere overture. Soon they leave and that is the last I hear from her for several years.

I realize I have made a decision that meant I would be subjected to the same life I had known now for almost ten years. I also knew it would get worse, just as it did for Cindy. I would be responsible for the cleaning and the laundry, as well as the other chores I already did. In my mind, I realized that for the next five years I would be doing time.

~.~.~.~

The beatings that I seemed to receive regularly have all but stopped. Things are calmer, however the verbal reminders continue as do the looks that linger. I was sure the change in the physical abuse had to do with my decision to stay. Still, it was the way that Elaine would ask for something that reminded me she was barely capable of holding back. Perhaps the presence of the construction workers also prevented her from lashing out.

John was there every morning at 6:30, waiting to start. I bring him a cup of coffee as instructed by Elaine. I offer him refills, watching him assemble the forms for the foundation. I see the look on his face when Elaine yells for me; it's uncomfortable for him. She's calling out for her coffee and his eyes fall to the cup in his hand realizing I'm her servant. A few weeks have gone by. I'm addressed as a "son of a bitch," words echoing from the other room. He sees me and smiles warmly, then he says,

"Eddie, I feel very bad for you. You're a strong boy and it makes me proud to know you."

His words are rewarding and my spirit lifts although my face stays the same. Shortly, our eyes release and I attend to my summons. Their "son of a bitch" is coming.

I'm focused at school, remembering the words I spoke to Elaine and Hank about my education. That is why I told them I would stay when my mother came asking for me. The classrooms are larger and there is a football field where games are played every Friday. I'm not permitted to stay, but I take my time anyway. Elaine is at work and Hank is on the road. Who will know?

This new surrounding is a fresh start for me. I have tempered the chip harbored on my shoulder and I'm making new friends. My mind is harnessed in this analytical state while utilizing these available moments, spending my time reflecting on the subtle incidents inside those white walls on Ninth Street as I walk toward school.

It begins with the autumn dew glazing my face in the early morning fog. It happens in a moment, as I exit the screen door my sister went flying through a few months before. That vision continues to haunt me and I wonder where she might be. This is my quiet time. It brings reality into focus and I feel the conflict from the tones in voices weathered the night before rising off my chest like the fog hovering above the path.

There are two semesters in Jr. High, which is new to me and feels important. I have gone to the next level in school, at home, and somewhere else, even on the street. The street is not existent as my walk is now away from the park. It's the same walk I had when I attended Wilson Elementary. Some of the kids remember me and I remember them. Most of the kids in my neighborhood now attend Smeadly, a school in south Santa Ana.

There's a school dance at the annex so I take a chance and ask if I could go. "If your work is all done," She says. I'm stunned as warm excitement fills me. This is a big deal! Somehow, I find out where the annex is and make my way there. Turns out it's near the police department off Civic Center. Walking, I take precautions, Civic Center Drive can be dangerous turf. Most students are dropped off by their parents, and most of them are dressed very nice.

Inside the big hall the lights are low. It's a party atmosphere, something I have never seen before. The music plays popular songs and a few brave the walk to the side of the room where the girls are huddled, ignoring us. I find the punchbowl and watch the others mingle. This, too, is new to me. I have never danced before so I watch, hoping I will catch on. Soon nine o'clock comes and it's time to leave. I didn't dance but I learned how to act.

Walking home, I keep aware of my surroundings. I stay off the sidewalk, instead choosing the side of the street that is dark, that way I won't be seen. In my neighborhood, that was safer. From behind me I hear the pipes of a low rider cruising up a few blocks back. I step behind a bush and wait for it to pass, contemplating my escape and wondering if they see me. Inside the early '60s Chevy I see four troopers with blue headbands. I won't be bothered as they didn't see me.

The next day at school, all the talk is about the dance. I stand in the circle and listen to guys remark about the hot chicks. I'm still learning to act.

It's Friday evening and Elaine comes home early from work. In a flash, she runs back out. Hank is in the hospital. I lie in bed, wondering what has happened, and hours go by before the phone rings. Roberta says he will be in the hospital for a while.

It was an accident while he was fueling: that's what he called it when they filled the tanks up on the big rig. The seals leaked as the acid was being pumped in and the fumes consumed his lungs, burning them intensely. I have a strange feeling about him being in the hospital, leaving me sad and wondering if he will be alright. This stretches my emotions thin and I'm torn between the thought of him being injured and the thoughts of him punching me in the back of my head. I give way to compassion; this helps me feel like part of the family unit. It feels good, I think, to come together, even if it is on the outskirts of the unit.

The damage to his lungs left him disabled and now he would be home permanently. The dynamic change in the household was intense. It seemed like weeks went by with him lying in bed. The recovery was long and he mostly slept. Now I had to be home right after school again. I understood why, and did so accordingly. We actually got along in the beginning and, once he was up and about he didn't mind me having some fun so I ran track. I really think he wanted a fresh start after I chose to stay with them. He was definitely making an effort.

February 9th, 1971, I wake up with the bunk bed shaking like crazy. Little Henry is in the top bunk, so I think he's horsing around. He's not. He yells, "Mom! Eddie won't stop shaking the bed!" It wasn't just the bed shaking. When the Sylmar quake hit in the early seventies, things changed. Our school was shut down, structurally condemned. We did split sessions at the high school putting an end to all sports activities and my after-school freedom.

Something else was happening too. Hank was restless and on several different medications. He developed a weird stare when he got angry and his eyes bulged. It wasn't long after this that we began to clash *hard* for reasons I couldn't explain.

I remember him actually timing me to and from school, telling me I had thirteen minutes or I was in trouble. Considering I had to ride all the way from Santa Ana High School now, it was almost impossible to do this. He would be waiting for me in the front yard sitting on the porch, reminding me he was in charge.

He helped with the house work and even did some of the cooking, but he was constantly angry and impossible to reason with.

The next year, we returned to Willard. With portable classrooms and a big field we found a way to make a school out of it. I resumed after school sports and rode my bike to school. In many ways, I found normalcy as long as I wasn't at home. Intramural football, track, and baseball were available and I was able to participate as long as all my work was done. With Hank's blessing, I worked my tail off, holding him to our agreement. Still, he was a loose cannon and I never knew when or why he would go off.

I'm up early and out the door. With my face in the breeze I peddle off, excited to be able to breathe aloud. This window of freedom is savored each morning, bringing peace to my struggling mind, helping me to contemplate what I can do to avoid the reoccurring incidents and actions. Each night it's the same thing. That dull-eyed look he gives me when I enter, bracing myself for the evening's episode – an exact repeat, if not for the dwindling space between us, filled by his raising anger.

Eventually and inevitably he snaps. I'm at the sink washing dishes from the evening's meal. The burnt orange grease from tonight's Hamburger Helper has left the skillet to find the surface absorbing the few remaining suds and leaving its ring against the white porcelain sink. He's picking at me for not practicing my clarinet enough. I hear his words but they don't register. He thinks I'm ignoring him but I don't mean too, I just want to get my hands out of the scalding water I'm required to wash with. Reaching for the towel to dry them off, I turn just in time to catch a glimpse of him closing in. He explodes with a series of swings, left-right-left! They catch me in my shoulders as I dip away out of his reach.

It's only a second or two before he is braced against the counter top, supporting his heavy frame, laboring to catch his breath. The sweat drools from his brow. His frustration is clear but his reasoning is odd. I look at him wondering how I can respond without amplifying this situation. He is ill, on medication for high blood pressure, and he stands in front of me with veins bulging off his temples. I'm caught between emotions as I wonder if this will trigger that heart attack Elaine's telling him about. I'm without answers.

The energy has shifted around the house. It was as if there was a huge secret being suppressed. Everyone was walking around with this sense of shock about them. Hank and Elaine's silence only amplified the sense of unease. Something was up, yet I didn't have a clue what it could be. For the first time, I could actually feel animosity toward Roberta from Elaine. It was almost a jealousy of sorts. Voices rose toward Roberta.

What is going on here? I wondered as weeks went by before it made sense. Then, one day, little Henry says to me, "You know that Roberta is pregnant?!"

They make arrangements for Roberta to move out into her own place a few miles away on Eleventh Street.

Early Saturday morning, I pack her belongings into the back of the '65 Chevy, secure the ropes, and let Hank know the truck is ready. We climb in and he drives over. I unload everything as I have orders from Elaine that Hank isn't to lift anything. Dynamics in the house have changed, leaving only little Henry and myself alone with a very nervous Hank, while Elaine works the three to eleven shift. Days turn into months and my disposition weathers like worn leather, my emotions are dry.

~.~.~.~

That chip I had resting on my shoulder had awakened. The last several weeks, I have absorbed Hank's regiment of slaps in the back of my head. Jarred loose is that attitude from the street I had tucked away. I slipped back into survival mode, packing the frustration away until I got out of the house, purposely leaving an hour early for school to play basketball before class, finding an outlet to release.

Consumed with anger, I was looking to take it out on someone, anyone.

Almost daily, there was a fistfight at P.E. All it took was a look; in the lunch line, or after school, perhaps even in class. It didn't matter. I would unload *anywhere*. The district's boundaries changed because of the earthquake and several Chicanos were transferred to our school. A few of them were my friends, but there were others I didn't know. This gave rise to a new pecking order, my skills from the street resurfacing as my persona emerges.

Recycled behaviors seeped from my pores and sprayed onto those around me, empowering me, bringing me attention and propping me up as I walked with a warriors face. No longer able to excuse my actions by laying them on the neighborhood, it was clear that I had developed a mechanism of empowerment similar to the days at Fremont. This mechanism, however, was driven by my home life, fueled by emotions of oppression and the unjustifiable advantages taken of me.

Life on the street again became my refuge, my escape, and the theater for attention to offset what I dealt with in an abusive home. Unfortunately, the chip jarred loose by Hank's overbearing presence also knocked me out of balance. I wobbled about, an angry fourteen year old adolescent, bitter in some ways and lonely in others. Anxiously, I waded through the days, the fist fights, and the aggression. I couldn't wait for this year to be over as it marked the end of the second of the five year term I signed on for.

Doing time.

Restricting Manipulations

It's now summer vacation, school has been out a few weeks and I'm already wishing it would start up again. I'm looking forward to September, when my freshman year will begin. Without school I'm literally locked down, similar to when I was younger and couldn't go anywhere.

Most teenagers are counting the days before school is out; I kept count of the days left before school would start again. Each week is like a continuous weekend that never ended. They roll one into the other and Elaine is in my face all day long.

It starts with her pathetic whine each morning for coffee. "Coffee...coffee...bring me my coffee." She thinks she's cute, calling out to be served in bed, as she lays sprawled in her new master bedroom, sheets pulled between her legs to cover her crotch. Little Henry is in their old room, separated by a pocket door. He sleeps in so I walk down the hall and around the long way. Two heaping spoons of sugar with cream for Elaine – Hank takes his black. He always says thank you. She says, "Bring me some toast."

This summer I get to paint the outside of their house canary yellow with white trim. "Is it ok if I get started with the painting?" I ask.

Hank says, "Why don't you wait for me?"

I say, "It's ok, I'll get everything ready." The reality is he can't exert himself but feels guilty I'm doing all the work. It's his pride.

Thinking out in front, I devise a plan to talk him into letting me play freshman football. He is grateful and appreciates my abilities and willingness to do these types of chores, and I know this is the right opening to bring it up, as he'll be pleased with me. As the week progresses, we begin to talk about it.

Little Henry is supposed to be helping but always seems to disappear. I don't mind, I can do this. Climbing to the eave's peek with a small bucket in hand and the wooden handle of the brush in my teeth, Hank comes over and steadies the ladder. We talk some more about football and he tells me of the days he played center. At the end of the day we take a break on the steps and we talk some more.

It feels good to be on these terms, and it reminds me of the times when we used to work on the cars before his accident. I remembered the end of the day when he would tell me I was a big help, it was like rubbing a puppy's belly and I couldn't get enough of it. He says he will need to fatten me up and I smile thinking he is going to let me play. Then he says he will have to talk to "the boss" first and I think to myself, it's a start.

The next morning, as always, I bring them their coffee. Dressed and ready for the day's painting, I enter and place their cups in the usual spots next to their bed and hand Elaine a plate with her toast. As I'm leaving, Elaine brings up the topic. She has no problem with it as long as I keep my nose clean and it doesn't interfere with my grades. Taking a bite of toast, she reminds me it is a privilege and she will take it away if I'm disobedient. My mind races to the last time I wasn't on restriction.

I'm always on restriction.

When she's finished, I say thank you and leave the room, equating "privilege" with the times they have reminded me that "I should be thankful they put a roof over my head."

I work extra hard, fueled by the thoughts of playing ball. I want this so bad. The entire house is finished and it looks great, well, as great as canary yellow could. Frank is across the street and walks over, admiring my work. He tells me it looks great, "You did a nice job." Hank shakes his head in agreement and I know he is proud of me. Inside I feel good as I'm hustling about, picking up the tools and paint cans. I'm wondering if maybe things will be better now, and I'm hoping I earned the privilege to play ball.

~.~.~.~

It's the 4th of July, exactly two years ago this day that my mother passed me on the street as I exited Mondo's market. Cindy did the ironing then, now I do. It's mid-morning and Elaine has finished her third cup of coffee. She nibbles at the buttered toast I prepared for her while plopped into the blue velvet sectional. I feel her looking at me as I pull the pant leg over the tapered end of the ironing board, keeping to my chore, sensing something bad is about to happen.

There's no work today, so she's dressed in her green nylon stretchy pants, the ones she wears on the days she isn't going to work. She has something planned, I know. Getting up, she walks past me with a methodical sway, entering the hall and disappearing momentarily. She calls for me so I leave the ironing board realizing she is in the hall bath. What now, I wonder. I scrubbed the bath this morning and I know it's perfect.

"Come over here," she says, her voice eerie and almost rhythmical. I walk closer, wondering what this is about. Her hands reach out toward my face to squeeze a blackhead. It hurts, but I stay still. She used to do this to Cindy and it was never a good thing, it left her scarred. Minutes go by and it seems like forever. She is still going at it and my face is burning. She

moves to another, then another. It's tortuous.

I'm feeling tedious and fatigued as she continues her pinching and squeezing. This time it's too much and I flinch. "Stand still, God damn it!" She squeezes harder and glares into my eyes, her brows drawn tight, warning me not to cross her. I just need a break and ask her but she won't stop and I'm flinching again. She begins to slap me about the head and face as my hands go up to protect myself. "Don't you raise your hands to me you little bastard!" Her nails dig into my neck, ripping open the flesh. Her hands grasp my neck and her nails pinch into me. She's trying to choke me. I just stand there and take it, my mind goes off and I don't even look at her. She hands me a bottle of methiolate and tells me to put it on my wounds.

With my eyes locked in the mirror, seeing only myself, I dab the glass rod applicator to my wounds, feeling the burn as the antiseptic stains my skin pinkish-red.

She leaves, shutting the door on her way out.

This is the next level, I think. She has never done anything like this before, not even to Cindy. Then again, maybe she has. It was many years ago, nearly ten, when I was in kindergarten. My hands barely reached the countertop as she poured the hot green liquid over my palms before telling me to turn them over, then more to stain the backs of my hands and wrists.

It was here, in this same bathroom, that she slung me across the floor into the wall telling me to scrub the floor again as the yellow toothbrush hit me in the shoulder. Locked in forever with a can of comet, my knees turned white from the cleanser. That was the first time my skin was stained.

The methiolate continues to burn as it dries, sealing the toxic violations marking my body.

Later in the day she tells me I'm on restriction and better keep my nose clean. I say nothing. She continues to remind me that I better do exactly as I'm told or I won't get off restriction for the rest of the summer. What she is really saying is I won't be able to attend football practice.

It's two weeks later on Sunday evening and I ask to enter their bedroom. Football practice starts the next morning, my restriction is supposed to end today.

"No, you have one more week to go, if you keep your nose clean and do as your told you can start practice then." Hank sits in silence as she speaks. The scabs on my neck have dried and they itch, soon they will fall off.

The following Monday I show up for practice. I'm behind and have never played organized football with pads and helmets. I have to explain that I missed the first week because I was on restriction. The coach curls his upper lip and tells me to stay out of trouble.

His eyes go to the pinkness in my skin where scars are forming. I turn and head to the field, embarrassed.

I work hard in practice each afternoon, running the drills, catching the ball, and learning the routes. I make sure I get home right afterwards to do my chores and help with dinner. When I return, Elaine is gone for work. The house is clean and Hank is helping out, even making little Henry pick up after himself. We sit at the table, a glass of milk is poured, and I eat. Hank fills my plate again, "We have to fatten you up."

Ever since I painted the house earlier in the summer he has been nicer to me. He seems pleased and supportive of me entering high school and playing football. Again, we are getting along.

It's "hell week," the last few days before school starts. We are down to our core team and I'm a wide receiver. I'm fast with good hands and excited to be part of the team. Friday comes, ending the long week with double practices. Today we get our pads. Walking home, I proudly carry my pads in one hand and my helmet in the other while wearing a practice jersey (we won't get our game jerseys for another week). Still, I've got my pads, and school starts on Monday. Approaching the house I see my Godfather, Mr. Lucio. He's out front hosing down his drive. He smiles and says, "Eddie, you're playing football? I'm so proud of you!"

It's Sunday night and I'm in my room getting prepared for

tomorrow: the first day of high school. I hear the echo warp from the back of the house. It's Elaine calling for me. I lay the brown shirt on top of the beige flares and hurry into their room.

They're both sitting upright on the bed; Elaine's eyes never leave the television. I can sense it's not good. Hank looks into sheets still bunched from a bed never made. Without looking at me he begins to tell me, in a strange tone, they have talked it over and decided I'm not big enough to play football. That they're worried I might get hurt. As his words form my spirit sinks. I'm stunned, feeling betrayed and knowing that isn't the reason. Wanting to convince them anyway, I tell them I will be fine but Elaine cuts me off, "You heard me, don't buck authority! You know better than to talk back!" I'm back on restriction.

Walking from the room, I hear Hank say, "Maybe next year."

Early the next morning as I walk to school, my mind wonders how I will explain this to my teammates. I worked so hard to earn these privileges. I gained four pounds in the last month and actually felt the pads on my shoulders and laced tight against my chest.

I felt betrayed. The little voice that talked in my head reminds me I should have known better. I wished I had never gone out because some of the kids will now think I'm a quitter. They didn't know what life at home was all about for me, and it's not like I could tell them. Worse was that

Elaine and Henry waited until I finished "hell week" and came home with my pads and helmet. I was embarrassed having to take them back on Monday in front of everyone, another cross to bear.

~.~.~.~

Enrolled in early morning typing and writing classes would get me out of the house with the sunrise. I could be up and gone before Elaine summoned for her coffee, and by the time I returned home she would be off to work. I took advantage of this schedule to avoid being in her path. Shortly after school starts, I find out she too is pregnant.

She had hidden it well. Only a month to go and I couldn't even tell she was pregnant. After the baby was born I couldn't tell she wasn't. What I could tell is that I was being trained to change diapers and warm bottles. The diaper pail got emptied each day and before I washed them I had to rinse out the yellow poop. I got up even earlier in the mornings to get ready, making sure there was a warm bottle for baby Erin before leaving.

Within a few weeks Elaine was back at work and Hank became Mr. Mom. I rushed home each day to relieve him from Erin, taking over as he caught his breath and dried the beads of sweat rolling off his forehead. I observed that this was too much for him. He was still ill and now fatigued, soon he would be agitated. I knew what that meant.

Although Elaine worked full time, she had her ways of catching up on the weekends for the confrontation I was dodging by avoiding her during the week. She had a little ritual when she got up and about, and I would get a late morning summons.

She called me into the bathroom where she stood posed and ready to do her work. Conditioned, I set my mind for the several minutes she would spend pinching each inch of my face, searching the pores and forcing them to bleed. "See, there was one." It was as if she enjoyed popping zits, many caused from the squeezing weeks before. I would squirm, and her constant picking left potholes in my face. If I would pull away she would slap me and tell me to hold still. So I tried to stand still and endure the pinching sensation, hoping I could withstand the pain until she tired, contemplating what would happen if I didn't. Eventually I couldn't take it and the assault on my head, neck, and back would take over.

Methodically, she would dig her nails into the sides of my neck, ripping deep gashes as she angrily stared into the mirror, locking her glare to my eyes. These were not scratches, these were wounds caused by the depth of her nail tips that resembled claw marks traveling four to six inches down my neck. Every weekend she seemed to make time for this specific and cruel ritual. When the bottle of methiolate was gone she replaced it with a bottle of iodine. Not liking the blue color it left on my skin, she replaced it with a bottle of mercurochrome, which she brought home from the hospital to treat the wounds for infection. My skin stained from the mercurochrome that I dabbed carefully along the wounds. It was wicked how she would look at me after her work was done and my neck was ripped open. Even more wicked were the fresh wounds over the old scars that now covered my neck and back.

These scars sealed into my body the toxic poisoning that infected my soul. Scars are only superficial: eventually they fade leaving no tell-tale signs of the broken spirit beneath. A broken spirit cannot nurture the soul and, in my eyes, one could see I had lost all hope. I was overwhelmed without options or alternatives. I learned to cope and I learned the art of toleration.

At school I would ignore the many questions asked as I did not want to mix the happy times with the sick actions of my aunt. There were other actions that were sick also, just in a different way. That Christmas, my gifts included several turtle neck shirts to cover the scars.

It has now been nearly two years since I received a letter or card from my sister. I remember the first and only one I received disappeared from my dresser shortly after it arrived. I never thought that they would keep my sister's letters from me, but that is exactly what happened.

Now that Hank was home he got the mail. Of course, Elaine was behind it, which I would find out later. He turned it over to her and she kept it from me.

I joined the marching band to get me out of the house on weekends, and for other events like the football games that were required. I learned to play the drums so I could be part of the pep band at basketball games. I would do *anything* to get me out of that house!

It was strange how Hank arranged for me to get my motorcycle license, which was very nice and I'm sure accommodating for them. This gave me clout at school because I was the only a freshman with a motorcycle. On the other hand, he would take it away all the time for no reason other than he was angry at the world. Even though I had earned the money and paid for it, he still signed for my license and provided the roof over my head, which he reminded me of frequently.

Frustrated with his debilitation, his agitation turns, again, toward me.

Shortly into the summer of that year I began rebelling from Hank and his ways. I stood in defiance as my sister had while he beat on me daily. The day finally came when he got pissed at me and, in an angry rage he threw me through the front screen, reminiscent of what Elaine did to Cindy on her final day.

The sensation that came over me as I picked myself up from the concrete sidewalk was unlike anything ever known to me before. It was a release of sorts, a sense of freedom, and a new ownership over my life. I could not believe how energized I was feeling. I just kept going as he called for me to come back, I ignored him. I was done putting up with his outbursts and slaps to the back of my head when my back was turned. Elaine's abusive ritual too, her nails marking my body with multiple scars, making my neck look like a road map.

He calls out to me again, "Get back here!" but I know he has miscalculated, his actions opening the way toward my exodus from their control. He calls out again and then says, "Go to hell then, you son of a bitch!"

Toward the park I go, but I stop as I approach that sacred place I haven't seen for some time. I am drawn to the canopy of my trees as these old friends call for me. To the edge I have walked and I feel the energy enclose me, embracing and welcoming me. Silently speaking with their great powers, my soul reaches for the highest branches as I feel lifted in a completely different and spiritual way. I have made the right choice.

I walked toward the park, wondering in my mind how I will live. Then, out of nowhere, is Jawbones' brother Jessie. We were always friends, even though one of his older brothers tried to corner me years before in the bathroom when I had ditched school and was running the streets.

Jessie said to go with him because he wanted to talk to his mom about it. As I went with him I appreciated the dinner they gave me and how they invited me to stay, but I didn't feel comfortable from the incident years before. They were very kind to me but I told them I had another place to stay. As the day went on I ended up at Roberta's, sleeping on her couch for the evening.

The smell of her house was full of filth with dishes that were weeks old just piled up. Cups with curdled milk and leftover fast food were stacked in the refrigerator. The bathroom shower had mildew throughout and the sink was black with germs. Clearly, all the years of watching Cindy and I clean had taught her nothing. She had never raised a hand to help and it was evident she lacked the skills to keep up her own home.

Elaine and Hank were going on vacation in a few days and so I just stayed there for a few weeks. Roberta now had her full time housekeeper and yard cleaner. She was barely home so I kept busy. Her house was a sty. The carpet was full of dried puppy poop from the litter that was born weeks before. I had to clean the carpets for days in the room in which she expected me to sleep on the floor.

The yard that had been overgrown was trimmed nice, and the bushes that bulged to heights of over twelve feet across the back of the yard had been tamed. The house was immaculate. By the time the Whitsett's re-turned from vacation, I was settled in and Roberta wanted me to stay with her. She said I could keep her house clean in exchange, of course!

Facing The Demon

It is Saturday, a day after Elaine and Hank returned from vacation. The afternoon's warm sun beats down onto the front of Roberta's house where I'm outside scraping the front porch, getting it ready to paint. Roberta tells me she is going to split because her mom is back and is coming over to talk. The smell of thinner is on me as I had been prepping and painting Roberta's house for days. I think about the rag I kept soaked with mineral spirits penetrating the back pocket of my jeans, it irritates the skin beneath. As Elaine pulls into the driveway, I glance toward the new pinto wagon with imitation wood panels on the side. Then my eyes go to the cigarette that dangles out of her mouth, and to the hands atop the steering wheel that have assaulted me countless times. I prepare my mind for the conflict I'm sure is about to take place.

Scanning my work she orders me into the house. Placing the paint brush into a milk carton with thinner I set my mind again to stand up to her and make my way into the house.

She is touring the rooms, inspecting the counter in the bathroom I now clean. Then, it's off to the kitchen where she marvels at the empty sink I scoured to make white and spotless. That strange sense of pride comes over me as I see recognition emerge on her face.

At first, I think it is because of my nice work, but then I realize it is value she sees. I'm *her* servant, not Roberta's, and she is here to take back what rightfully belongs to her.

Sitting on the couch, she begins to speak. I walk to the center of the room and stand across from her. She comments on how nice Roberta's house looks. My stance is defiant as I don't need her compliments; I have made up my mind. She begins to tell me what is going to happen and to get my stuff because we're going home. Then I tell her,

"I have decided I'm not going back."

Her face reddens with rage. She continues to get angry, but I notice that she hasn't gotten up to hit me. I wonder only for a moment before I realize she is afraid to attack me, as she is here by herself. I go on to explain to her I'm tired of being beat on and that I do not deserve it. She threatens that if I don't go she will call the police and they will take me to juvenile hall.

"That's fine with me. I'm tired of putting up with everything and I think it will be better that way."

As I tell her this I realize she is completely pissed, her face contorts and she rises tall as she sits, "I'm warning you, God damn it!"

"I've made up my mind."

As I state this, I go back out to the front porch and continue prepping the walls. I hear her call the police telling them I'm a delinquent. The rag in my back pocket continues to burn my skin as I scrape the wooden window casing. I'm proud to stand up for myself.

When the officer arrives, I follow him inside and Elaine starts in. He stops her and tells her to calm down. It's clear he doesn't like her demeanor, and the words she's used to describe me makes him aware of her offensive nature. He then asks me to wait outside for a minute as he wants to talk to Elaine by herself. He has taken control of the situation and I feel even more empowered.

Several minutes passed before he comes out to me and we talk. He looks me in the eyes and he says, "I don't like that woman." I just smile. Then he explains my options and encourages me to give it one more try as it will be better than juvenile hall.

"I will make it clear to her that they're not to hit you any more but, just in case, take this card and if they do call this lady. She'll be able to help you." I'm eager to please the officer so, in a leap of faith, I agree, hoping that – maybe – things will be different.

The drive home is made in silence, no words. Elaine is speechless as she realizes I now know of a new empowerment and have just witnessed her being put in check by the police officer. I have resolve, my mind has changed and I will not tolerate things as before.

For the first few weeks Hank stayed away from me, mostly because Elaine had talked to him about the cop's attitude. Neither of them was aware he had slipped me the card which I kept hidden away like a card shark. This was my ace in the hole, just in case.

~.~.~.~

Toward the end of the summer things start to heat up again but this time I had a new tactic. When Hank would come directly at me, I would step to the side of him. He was big and carried a lot of extra weight, so when he would get angry I just used it against him. First I would stay out of his reach. Then if he did get close enough to me, I would just slip whatever he threw.

It was almost opposite to when I was little and had to deal with the kids on the street. They had no idea that a man of 260 pounds was beating on me, so they couldn't hurt me. Hank and Elaine had no clue that I was in fistfights daily at school. I could tag someone three or four times and step away without catching return fire. Although I didn't hit back, I did slip everything he could throw at me. This frustrated him and he started backing off as it was only embarrassing that he couldn't hit me unless he caught me at the sink. A few times, while doing dishes, he would sneak up from behind me at clobber me in the back of the head. I would just escape if this happened and leave him huffing and puffing. Still, I was tough and could take his assaults from behind.

When school started my sophomore year I decided to take action. I was concerned with the intensity of the violence at home. They were both sick and twisted people, and I was becoming stronger and less likely to put up with it. Once again, they took football away from me after I went through "hell week," and, once again, Eddie Whitsett was getting looks from the other kids. This time, though, they had seen the scars on my back and neck in the locker room. It was clear that something was going on. A few teachers even inquired, but I wouldn't talk. I did finally confide in my band instructor that I needed to get away and talk to the lady whose name was on the card, and that is when intervention began.

Her name was Karen. When I first stopped by the police station she was busy with another person. I waited as long as I could but soon I had to leave because the window of time set aside to see her was gone. As I was leaving she came running down the hall, catching me before I reached the stairs. We talked for a few minutes and then she asked me if I could come back another day. I explained to her I had to be home right after school and didn't know how I could see her, but she said she would take care of it.

Watching her walk back to her office down the long wide hall with polished vinyl floors and light walls lit with the brightest lights, I wondered what would come of today's meeting. I turned and slipped away.

I had defied my aunt and uncle to the greatest extreme. Now I would see how things played out and figure out if, in fact, there was a way to peacefully transition from the hell I lived in.

It's now a few days later that same week. I just arrived at my second period class and am getting settled in. Shortly after role call, a messenger is at the door with a summons for me to go see the principal.

This is interesting, I think to myself, *I'm probably going to get in trouble for the fight I had yesterday at P.E.*

I follow the messenger to the principal's office and am told to have a seat. After about ten minutes, a man comes out and asks me into his office. In my mind I'm thinking this is not a disciplinary issue; that something else is up. Then it dawns on me: the wheels have started in motion and the lady from the police department must have contacted the school.

The vice principal asks me into his back office and shuts the door. He is a tall man with a quiet, business-like demeanor. "Eddie, I have been contacted by the Santa Ana Police Department in regards to some domestic violence issues…"

He goes on to explain that the police department had asked them to help accommodate my schedule so I could see the counselor, the lady on the card.

Each Tuesday and Thursday I was to leave before fifth period and walk down to the police station. There, Karen and I would sit and talk, reviewing the week's events, filling her in on the incidents and how they began.

Never once did I tell her or show her the scars and wounds on my neck and back as I wanted her to believe me at face value. This was important to me, as I had always been treated as a liar or thief by my aunt and uncle. I saw this as "above board" play. Little did I realize at the time, this need of mine to be validated would drag out and complicate the process immensely.

I explained to her how things were getting worse and how I was afraid I would lose it and go off on them if it didn't stop soon. I was getting bigger and could handle myself on the street. It wouldn't be long before something snapped.

We met regularly during the first semester and her insight helped me cope. She would give me tips on how I could defuse the situation, but it seemed I was already doing everything she suggested. Still, just having someone to talk to gave me strength and helped me carry on.

Unspoken Protection

On the other side of the coin, I had my street life to deal with. On campus big changes are in the air and it seems as though the school is in transition. There are still fights and jumpings, but it's different, not like a year before when it was six on one. We had our rumbles and uproars but the torch had been passed and the athletes had made a stand. There were some big boys that weren't going to stand by and watch. They had seen enough and the gang bangers had been put on notice.

The senior class was full of giants: giants of all colors and they came together to send a message of unity. Football players and wrestlers had made up their minds that they owned the school, and there would be no more racial incidents without consequences.

Although the tension was less, security had increased and there were more guards on campus, which also included patrolling the grounds around campus. Don, an upper classman, was jumped on the way to his car one afternoon, big mistake. He was an all state CIF champion wrestler. Methodically, he broke arms and busted knees. It was five on one.

They should have brought ten.

This was a huge turnabout and was probably the biggest event to change the tide.

Several times that year the school would be shut down for days because of rioting. Someone would get jumped in the bathroom and the doors from the nearest classrooms would open up and out would pour athletes.

Athletes of *all* colors.

Nothing went without retaliation. The school seemed completely out of control. It was ugly. One thing happened and it was like a war zone. Students were running off campus – actually, *fleeing* would be a better word – and the school would be shut down for the rest of the week.

Being in the marching band had its benefits, mostly getting me out of the house with an activity that both Elaine and Hank approved of. It also opened the door to my first relationship, Sherry, a friend and confidant. She worried about me and wondered why I kept my scars a secret. I told her I didn't want to use them against my aunt and uncle. With two years left, I could weather the situation and then I would be out.

Her best friend, Terri, asked me if I would be interested in helping her father clean his new restaurant. Eager to have an excuse to earn extra money and get out of the house, I agreed and sought permission. It was more of a social event than anything, but it turned out to be another defining moment in my life.

Arriving on my motorcycle early in the morning, I enter the Top Hat restaurant located atop a gas station in south Santa Ana. A handful of other boys from school are there also. Mr. Peace, Terri's dad, brings us into the kitchen and points to the walls and ceilings that need to be scrubbed clean of grease that has built up over many years.

I go right to work, grabbing a ladder and attacking the ceiling. Four hours later, it sparkles. Four hours later, I have cleaned more than the other five boys put together. Elbow grease is what it was called. That special cleaner that doesn't come in a can or bottle, that comes from years of practicing the technique of scrubbing.

The end of the day comes and I know that her father is really pleased. We all line up to get our pay. In front of everyone he makes a big deal out of my work comparing what I did to all of them. Then comes the reward: he pays me *double*.

Recognition goes a long way, especially when you're starved for it, but it's the *admiration* that stays with you. I earned his respect, but he also gave me acknowledgement in front of my peers, validating and inspiring me. This gesture prodded me to carry on and to look outside the shell of those white walls on Ninth Street.

~.~.~.~

There was a day in late spring where the air was cool and the morning sun still seemed warm. I was with my girlfriend, Sherri; we had been together for most of that year. Holding hands, I was walking her to class when I saw a kid that I played baseball with in little league at El Salvador park.

I hadn't seen him since he went to a different middle school, but I still thought of him as a friend. I gave him a "what's up" nod and in return he gave me a smirk. I understood his actions were about the racial tension more than it was about me, but still, he wasn't cool about it and his smirk became a stare down. Being with my girlfriend it was best that we just kept walking. His actions surprised me as this was the first time anyone I knew from the park or from my neighborhood had acted this way toward me. Usually, I would expect this from the guys out of Delhi or Cross Warner

That same day after fifth period, I came walking out the main entrance of the old building and down the stairs into the lunch area. There was Eddie O with his gang. Obviously, he was there to jump me and it came fast.

Coming right up to me, with no words spoken, he threw a right cross. I slipped his punch and, naturally, I returned a direct shot to his jaw and knocked him down. I hit him solid with a good right hand straight and he didn't come back. The next guy came at me with a flurry of over hands, but most didn't get through because I was giving up ground. Unfortunately for me, I was fighting backwards up the stairs, back into the building. As one guy would roll off, another would come at me with no time wasted. They were like a well oiled machine, synchronized and almost choreographed.

I was already through the fourth dude and catching shots to my chest. For the most part, I was holding my own and putting up a good fight, but I had fought my way up a second flight of stairs and I took some hits to get out of the corner. I got thrown down the stairs, but I found my feet and continued throwing blows, fighting them off. I was determined to get back outside where there might be some help.

The concrete steps to the building were in sight and, this time, I leaped off them as I didn't want to lose my feet again. I'm now through seven and, as it goes, the biggest and baddest goes last. In my mind I'm thinking, where the fuck is somebody? Since it's fifth period, all my friends are in sports so they're in the locker room unaware. Besides I was still a loner, but I'm thinking that *somebody's* got to be watching. What about Danny? He was just with me and he's always talking like he's somebody. He's a punk. He ran like a punk and left me on my own. This dude in front of me is big with a big chest and here he comes. I'm still ready to go but I'm getting worn out. What happened next was stunning.

From out of nowhere, Bear (Bobby's street name) comes flying over my right shoulder. Bear hits this dude so hard he is knocked backwards into two other vatos and the three of them bounce like bowling pins. The looks on their faces are priceless. Bear is the sergeant of arms of FxTroop, he controls all of the park at El Salvador.

Why is he stepping in for this white boy? It was all there in their faces. I didn't recognize these guys. They were from Second Street, farther south down Raitte. He tells them with his hand signal it's over. They step back following his orders for the time being. He looks at me straight up, "You ok?" he asked.

"I'm alright." We check off and that's it for that day.

People are standing around, eyes big, all trippin'. I did well to keep my feet and put up a good fight. I see no friends, only faces that I recognize. I realize I'm different than these people looking on, and I also realize that there are a lot of confused gang bangers wondering what just happened. To have someone like Bear step up sent a message of association. I was from his turf, his hood. These guys were peripheral members that didn't realize who I was, but now they did. I had unspoken protection as I belonged to the streets and always had respect from Bear, Louie, Pete and Gary. They ran the turf.

For weeks after that I knew I was marked. I also knew why I got jumped, the main reason being the pressure created by acknowledging Eddie O in front of his associates. It put him on the spot and, although he recognized me, he had to prove that he didn't claim a white boy. Because of his status, a reputation his older brothers, the "Veteronos," had started years before, the last thing he could do was show any friendship to someone other than brown. As the street goes, you didn't get any deeper than his "familia."

I didn't like the fact that I was attacked for merely saying hi. Who would have thought? However, the dynamics of the hood we lived in dictated this behavior. Eddie O had to save face or explain.

The contradiction was that Bear, who had all the clout, put loyalty first. Regardless of my color, he took a chance, a big chance. He claimed me and sent the message that I no longer stood alone and, in doing so, he was defying the defining boundaries most gang bangers knew. This went back to my first days in Fremont when I faced the entire school as the only white boy, and when I faced the pecking order that constantly evolved, and the unending challenges I dealt with just for being white.

Bear, Pete and Louie were there when I beat the kid in the park in front of everybody. They were there just smiling and watching. Little did I realize the respect they had for me. I had never even thought about it, but then it all made sense. Pete was always smiling at me during P.E., while he and Gary would be kickin' it in their kakis and white T-Shirts each day, as I would engage with some "back seat rider" with something to prove. I realized no one ever jumped me. It had always been held to a one-on-one fight even though there were plenty of numbers around. Clearly, this had been going on longer than I realized. It just took that one defining moment and the protection surfaced. It would be a week or so later when this incident would spill over into my home life.

Like any organization, when something like that happens, there must be answers. I can't tell you if there was ever a meeting called. I'm sure, however, that the discussion came up. Bear took a huge chance and, although I didn't get jumped again, I still had my share of daily battles.

After that day, I dealt with peripheral static from other bangers. Another kid from Second Street liked to shadow me with a handful of bangers. They had their time all coordinated but for some reason they just liked to shadow me. It wasn't long before I realized it was their attempt to intimidate. The frustrating element for them was I didn't care. I didn't fear him, I just stayed smart. I made sure I wasn't in a place they could get to me and I stayed my course.

Again this situation had amazing dynamics. Bea Ashby was his grandmother, and she was also one of my angels. She was a very special lady to me and I felt her compassion and concern for me. She lived across the street from me and was Frank's wife. I was the only kid in the neighbor-hood she would let into her house.

I remembered seeing this kid being brought over to her house one day. He didn't want to be there. His behavior was typical of a pouting 15 year old. I just observed him realizing that a lot of what happens on the street has nothing to do with what home life is about for these kids. His mom would have whipped his butt if she knew what he was up to.

Later that week, I'm being yelled at by Hank as he is upset over something I had done. It has to do with the time I took returning after a school event. I was fifteen minutes late. As I'm in his room with Elaine, little Erin is now walking and has begun to jump up and down on their bed. As he continues to jump I stand nearby focusing on him so in case he was to lose his balance and fall I could catch him. I must have not responded be-cause Hank from behind punches me with his fist in the back of my head.

As I fly forward, Erin and I make head to head contact and he bounc-es off the bed into the wall and screams. I snap. I have lost all ability to restrain myself as I know how hard my head is. I have been thrown into lockers at school head first and I have knocked guys silly with head butts during fights. This weapon of mine had just been unleashed on the little baby I have diapered, bottle fed, and played nanny to for the last eighteen months. Now in a state reserved for the street, I open up on Hank.

I beat him with the fury I have held pent up inside for years. He is hit in the face over and over and beat down to the ground with such anger and intensity in my rage. This goes on like a street fight for several minutes until Elaine finally jumps on top of me and they both are sitting on my back. As they let me up they stare at me like I'm a monster. For the first time I have allowed myself to let go and tears run down my face as they ask me, wanting to understand who I have become.

I rip open my shirt and I show them the welts on my chest from the street fight earlier in the week and tell them they have no idea what I deal with. I further tell them never to hit me again and never cause me to hurt Erin like they did. They stare at the ring marks left on me and try to explain how they had no idea what I have gone through, as though that excuses their actions.

That was the last time that Hank ever put a hand to me. He realized he could not handle me by himself and, even with the help of Elaine, I could have hurt them both. The one thing I didn't want to happen had now occurred and I must live with it. Even though I've been beaten and abused horrifically, I never wanted to turn violent against them. Perhaps it was my way of tempering myself; for being thankful that they gave me a place to live and a roof over my head, a reason to be civilized.

The rules have changed.

~.~.~.~

My sessions continue and I explain that things have changed in the house. Karen is informed about the fight and I express my concerns. Now that I have unleashed my demons, I may not be able to control them in the future. I look to her for the help I'll need to solve this dilemma, but she is without a solution. We continue to wait it out. School will be out soon and maybe we can make a move then.

A Walk Out Of Hell

When Easter vacation came along, I was not able to attend my meetings with Karen. This resulted in her calling the house and trying to speak with Elaine. Elaine told her exactly where to shove it and, after she hung up the phone, I heard her call for me.

I was out in the living room, aware that she had just spoken to Karen from the Santa Ana P.D. I could hear her as she opened the pocket door between her room and little Henry's and stomped through his room into the hall, out toward the living room where I stood. In my mind I was hoping she would understand that I was looking for resolution, not conflict, but could tell this would not be the case. She rushed toward me, slapping at my face with a cigarette in her mouth. I stood there as I normally would, just taking the assault, searching my mind for that place I had learned to go during these moments. That place that allowed me to ignore the onslaught and heartfelt pain of her ignorance.

Like a baboon in a full charge, she surged toward me with a cigarette dangling out of her mouth, she snorts, "This will teach you to buck authority!"

Her left hand grabs at my face and she digs her nails into my cheek, grasping a handful of flesh. She twists her fingers and my skin is torn open. I just stare at her with disappointment. She beats me about the left side of my head, screaming, "Wipe that smirk off your face you bastard!" I am numb to the pain. I am without response. I just stand there and take it, defying her brutality. Again she rips at my neck.

I give it to her to do as she pleases.

Once she finished – which meant once she had no more strength to continue – she walked away, spewing things like, "That will teach you to buck authority you little bastard!"

Into the bathroom I went, to wash blood from my wounds. Applying the folded washcloth to the tears in my neck so the bleeding would stop, I realize that, this time, she has really cut me deep and that the wounds will not stop bleeding on their own. As I stand at the sink with the hot water running, my mind is mesmerized with thoughts that I'm only doing time and that I can get through this. I must not break nor shall I allow her the satisfaction of knowing my pain. Aside from the day I beat Hank to the ground, it has been six years since they have seen me cry, and that was only because the judge made me come back to live here. Ever since I was small, I just looked at them, puzzled by their actions. Now, I no longer even do this, as I'm smarter than to think she is confused. I know she is both sick and brutal: a bad human being. I'm tired of her and I know that, soon, this will all be over.

~.~.~.~

It's late in the following week before I resume my meetings with Karen and she is aware things did not go well. Again, I omit the details of the beatings and make sure my turtle neck is pulled high enough to cover the scars and fresh wounds, still tacky with bodily fluids,that continue to drain. Karen confides in me that she's limited in what she can do, short of removing me from the home. With only two months of school left, we agree that I would weather the situation until then.

At school, my girlfriend, Sherry, keeps account of the newest scars as she picks the scabs from the older ones on my neck. She feels bad for me and I appreciate that, but I'm tough and know I'll get through this.

The awards banquet for the band is going to be held later this week. The next few days are consumed by the realization that I'm going to be the only kid without his parents there.

It's Thursday evening and I arrive early to the Elks Lodge. I notice many of the other members in the band are there, most of them with their parents. I had told Elaine about it but she did not care to attend, so I was the only member without a parent to represent them. I sat with Sherry and her mother. Feeling out of place and awkward, I tried my best to play off that I'm fine when, deep inside, I'm ashamed to be by myself.

Sitting at the long banquet table with a white turtleneck shirt pulled high, I feel discomfort at the scabs being tugged at by the fabric. The lights dim and the presentations begin. To my surprise, I'm called up over and over again to receive honors and awards for this last year's events. I had no idea this was coming and felt overwhelmed at first. Then, I feel pride as the parents and my peers begin to applaud. The realization of this acknowledgment is exhilarating and my girlfriend's eyes meet mine. Sherry had been such an incredible friend these last eight months and we had grown so close. The thoughts of being by myself again run through my mind as I look out at the crowd of several hundred and understand why I'm worthy of this acknowledgment.

Still, deepest regret remains inside as I think if Elaine and Hank could have been here they would have been so proud of me. What a lost opportunity.

Later that evening, as I arrive home with my arms full of awards and an elected office for the following year, I wonder what they would think as I let myself into the darkened front door. Entering the back part of the house where they sit in the den, I place the awards on the coffee table in front of them. Elaine asks me to get her coffee and I automatically attend to it. When I return, they stare at me with an amazed look on their faces. Obviously they're stunned.

"We had no idea this was such a big event." Hank feels the need to apologize for not making it and Elaine seems confused. They both show me, through their expressions of perplexity, that they are actually proud.

I say, "I wish you could have been there."

As I walk down the hall to my room, sadness comes over me. Tears fall from my eyes as I wished they could have seen me being honored for all my hard work. I was being acknowledged in a way that I had longed for all these years; just a *chance* to prove to Hank and Elaine that I was worthy.

~.~.~.~

It is now a few weeks into the summer months and, needing to keep busy, I offered to tear out and install a new kitchen floor. This is a big project and I'm in my third day of scraping the old carpet tiles that are stuck to the sub floor. The black rubbery glue is hard to remove but I'm determined to do a good job. My jeans are too tight as I'm growing out of them and will not get anything new until school starts again. I'm wearing a thin white t-shirt and no shoes. I have spent hours on my hands and knees scraping.

The phone rings and I can hear Elaine telling Karen to butt out or she will sue her. The phone slams down and she storms into the living room, calling me from the kitchen. As I approach her with my filthy jeans and skimpy thin t-shirt, she begins her verbal assault.

She is standing in the dining room and tells me to come out there. I put down the scraper I'm using to remove the black sponge rubber that has stuck to the sub flooring. Getting off my knees, I begin to walk out to her, knowing what's coming.

She starts to yell but, soon, her anger is ignited by my pre-disposed realization that I'm finished. She must sense this. I stand there as she begins her assault on my face and ears and eventually my neck.

The blows to my face and head subside as she weakens with exhaustion. She digs her nails into my neck as she has done so many times before, trying to rip open the scars that remain from the times she has done this in the past. I feel the blood running down my neck. The back of my right ear is torn from her nails digging in so deep.

"When you're done doing this to me, I will be leaving here."

When she raises her hand, I can see my blood on her nails. Her fingers are filthy. The same hand now grabs a fistful of my hair and she is pulling at it as if ripping the stuffing out of a cushion. I stand there and she slugs me with her right fist on the side of my face. I continue to stand there. My ears are ringing as I look her in the eyes, knowing I will never be hit again after she's done.

"This will be the last time you put your hands on me. I want you to know this."

My statements are as methodical as hers were the day she painted my hands green in Kindergarten; as specific as her nails that dug into my neck and back; as real as the iodine she provided to treat my wounds over the years.

"As soon as you are done, I will walk out that door and I won't be coming back."

I can feel her energy; she is breaking and is without the ability to continue. The tide has turned and, even though she is reaching as deep as she can, there is nothing left. I have done to her what she has been trying to do to me for years.

I have broken her spirit.

As she slows down, huffing and puffing, the rage in her face turns to exhaustion. She removes what is left of the broken cigarette from her mouth. "You are not going anywhere, you bastard," she breathes. Inhaling like a fiend begging for a breath, she walks into the back part of the house.

I turn and walk out the door.

~.~.~.~

This afternoon, the sun is hot and the pavement is blistering as I walk from Ninth Street toward the police department. I didn't bother putting on shoes, as I promised I would be gone when she was done. My jeans are tight fitting, about a size too small, but I just walk on as I head toward the civic center. I can feel the afternoon breeze on my face. It feels good on my wounds and breaks through the stale air from the smoggy day as I diligently continue on, thinking I may spend the next few years in juvenile hall or wherever you go as a minor.

It seems like every house along the way has a story. As if I'm being cheered on by the silence of the empty street, I feel only encouragement to continue. The first thing I feel as I walk from the porch is the realization I will never be going back. The neighbor's jeep is in their drive. Nellie is not home, but I know she is with me. I can feel her support.

Across the street, I see the front door of the Lucio's, my Godparents, as I cross the yard that I have tended to for years and the plum tree near the curb where I placed the trashcans each week. I glance quickly toward the park, really only to catch my last glimpse of the trees several houses down – the canopies that have sheltered and comforted me all these years. I glance at Frank's house, the man that gave so much to me. My "Angels," all of them, I leave behind today. I know they will always be with me, though, and I feel energy beneath me affirming my departure.

It is as if with each step I feel stronger as I go. Then I see Butch's house, my friend, the quiet one who lifted weights with me. His parents always smiled, encouraging me. I'm energized again. I pass the small well near the dirt lot that I used to retrieve scraps from to build my first go-carts. At the corner I turn right, seeing more and more familiar sights, all vibrant, all saying, "It's time to go, Eddie."

Right on Pacific, glancing at everything one last time, being empowered over and over again. Left on Civic Center, past Bristol; I look but see no one familiar. I march forward diligently, with purpose and desire to begin a new life.

As I pass the Santa Ana Bowl my pace picks up with intent and determination. I will never go back there, regardless of the circumstances that I may face. Soon, I'm nearing the large steps of the police department. I slow down, look up, and say to myself, "It is time."

My heart beats with the knowledge that I have done all I can.

I have tolerated too much and I have been worn too thin. My efforts were exhausting. My spirit hardened like slate under the pressure of the world for all my sixteen years. Or has it been centuries?

Once in the station, I feel uneasiness come over me. I have entered a realm of the unknown as I look to see if Karen is in her office. She is there, on the phone, and anxiously signals me to sit down while she finishes up.

"I knew you would be here," she states with a concerned look on her face. I read that she realizes this is the moment of truth and that we must move forward. Still, she asks me what I will do and if I will reconsider going back. I answer, no, I will not go back, even if it means going to juvenile hall. She gets up and asks me to follow her to a table outside of her office.

As I sit there, she passes by me to get her supervisor, Sergeant Palmer, and she soon returns with him. Staring hard into my face he is bothered. He thinks I'm wasting his time.

"I have heard all about your situation and if you would just keep your mouth shut this stuff wouldn't happen," he states.

I'm amazed that he has said this, as he has not even asked me a question. I don't understand how *I* have become the bad guy. He shakes his head and walks away to his office behind me. Karen now looks at me surprised not knowing what to say. I look back with wonder.

My thoughts are interrupted by the feeling of two giant hands upon my shoulders. They shake uncontrollably. The collar of my shirt is being pulled back and I feel the cotton soaked with dried blood being pulled as it tugs against my open wounds.

Slowly, my shirt collar is being pulled down and my neck is being examined as these giant hands continue to tremble. I hear the voice of the man that had just reprimanded me say gently, "Take off your shirt, son."

Looking up to see Sergeant Palmer's eyes meet mine, I sit tall. As my shirt comes off and he sees my neck and back for the first time, his eyes well up with tears and he lifts me out of my chair.

"Come here son," he says as he guides me over to his office. "No, you sit in my chair. How long has this been going on and did Karen ever see this?" He asks. She shakes her head no.

"He has never shown me this before," she states. I realize that he understands what I have been going through and is there to help me. I also realize that he now looks at me with admiration. He understands my strength, realizing that I never took the easy way out.

He asks me if there is anywhere I can go and I tell him either one of my grandmothers will take me. We call, and they are both willing, but we agree it would be better to go with Grandma Hansen.

The arrangements are made and there is only one detail left. Karen says she will call my aunt and uncle.

"No! *I* will do that," the sergeant states.

The phone rings and Elaine answers.

"This is Sergeant Palmer from the Santa Ana Police Department. We have Eddie here and I have seen what you have done to him. You disgust me!

"Eddie will be coming by to get his belongings. I want you to hear this from me directly. Should I get a call of any sort that you have even said one word to him, that you have threatened him or touched him in any way, I will personally be in your home. There will be so many police cars in your front yard that your head will be spinning! I will arrest you and I will take you to jail. Is that understood?"

Afterthoughts

Today I'm Free, Or Am I?

Exoneration is a strange feeling, more so when it involves a shift in power. Situational authority had me harnessed to circumstances that were crippling, with restrictive manipulations and devastation to my social growth and identity.

Though toleration was one key to my survival, finding the appropriate solution to my dilemma left me desperately searching for resolve.

With the help of Many, I found my way out. It was the validation from these Many that kept me going, seeking something *right* while submerged in *wrong*.

How does one escape the confines of control and abuse unscathed? One doesn't. So, resolving the circumstances of the situation did not free me from the bindings of learned behaviors: it only unlocked the shackles of another's control.

I'm but *one* that has walked this path of despair filled with moments that impacted my decisions as I moved forth, taking with me the tools in my shed to use only as I knew how. Understanding those tools was my blessing and learning to use them has been my journey.

The Morals Of My Story

As a child I learned a phrase,

"And the moral of the story is…"

Every story has a moral, so is it that I applied that rule to my life as well. But what is life if not a story? Blessed with a gift of insight, I walked my path with eyes wide open. I listened to the sound of the wind in the leaves, I heard the rain when it fell hard, and I smelled the warmth as it dried into the air leaving it fresh for us all to share.

Oppression led to observations and observations became my entertainment. Situational circumstances placed me within a limited realm controlled by an authority that saw my sister and me as tools, as less than equals, for we were orphans and orphans "should be grateful to have a roof over their heads."

Abuse taught me endurance: to endure neglect, to endure ignorance, and to endure the pain from punches and kicks, slaps and straps, and smacks to the back of my head, all, "for good measure."

I learned to flinch at a raised hand as it meant I should brace myself for the impact soon to follow. The impact: which is exactly that, an impact to my life and way of thinking, and on my ability to process and react. I pulled away out of reach so others could not hurt me, delaying my ability to socialize, to identify and be normalized.

Anger taught me to absorb what I must at the moment, which is what I did as a small child. I absorbed their anger as it saturated me, eventually learning anger of my own, and the art of lashing out as taught to me by them.

Intimidation also tainted my ways, for I learned as a small child that you will strive to do whatever you can to please a scary man. I took this tool with me as I grew and misused it too. Just as it was taught to me, I taught this to others and misused it to gain attention and to hide my insecurities.

I learned about inequalities in the eyes of others. Just like oppression, it is about ignorance. It is about insecurity, selfishness, and control. Mostly, it is about *fear of the unknown*. I learned that racism is about numbers more than it is about the color of one's skin. I learned that no matter what color you may be, there are plenty of people that are colorblind and will love you endlessly.

I learned that as time goes by, people change and so does the world. Each day we grow in mind, spirit, and body taking with us our lessons, our hurts, and our scars. As with time, our lessons evolve to choices. Hurts stay buried unless expressed and our scars fade away sealing our pain, absorbing it from our skin as it melts into our soul forever.

"Do as I say not as I do." For this I did as they said, knowing they were doers of things that should not be done. I did what I learned from those outside the walls of that house, from the neighbors who smiled at me; who sent me love and compassion secretly with small gestures.

I learned empathy for others who had less, for I was "less" until I knew more. Then, my empathy turned toward the ones that oppressed me, beat me and scarred me. I turned my heart to the same ones that said, "You are to be seen, not heard," because I realized I didn't need to be heard by them. There were others that saw my pain and sent me love, for they did not need to hear me, as the look in my eyes told them everything.

I learned compassion standing from afar seeing a man beat for his rude remarks by an angry father protecting his sons: compassion for the same man that beat me. He, too, stood there alone with no one to help him as he absorbed the blows. I learned compassion, for even the evil deserve to be understood. It is the ignorance they carry forth that represents them today.

I learned toleration for circumstances and grew to understand that physical pain is nothing when compared to a broken spirit. I learned to protect my spirit from anyone that tried to hurt it. I learned to honor my spirit and to listen to its tiny voice there to guide me.

I learned patience for the situation and the value of time, as it does march on. With each heartbeat, so goes another second of life, taking me toward the future that, eventually, would be my resolve to the problems at hand and the realization that I was only "Doing Time."

Mostly, what I learned was love. For me, it was not served on a silver platter or spoon fed to me by my mother, for she was not a part of my life. Love was not expressed through the physical touch, for love should not leave your body stained, battered or bruised. It was not expressed with a pat on the back or a warm hug or even hearing the words, "I love you," as I did not hear those words - except from my sister - and the pats on my back were violently delivered by a closed fist leaving knots that ached for days.

Love is what I learned from an old man across the street who could find a way to share his time with a neglected and battered young boy, teaching him with guidance, not anger.

Love is the lady next door who stood at her sink washing dishes with peace in her eyes and a smile on her face that illuminated the room like a framed picture. Love was the warm sandwich offered to the timid child that stood outside her door when he was hungry.

Love is about the family across the street stepping up and baptizing me; my Godfather who opened the door for sports and touched my heart with encouragement.

Love is about a perfect stranger standing up for me as my aunt accused me of being a thief when I wasn't. Regardless of her cruel and outrageous actions, the stranger's gesture is what stayed with me long after.

It's about a teacher that cared enough to take a few boys across town to enlighten them about a world they had no idea even existed, broadening their mind to expand the horizon past the ghetto they grew up in.

It's about a coach that understands the importance of giving his time so a kid - one like me - still gets to play even though he couldn't make practice.

Love is about the many people who took a moment to make up that difference; the gap in my life. When I was young it was the neighbors who sent me love. Through their love I learned right from wrong, I assessed and compared and I learned to know better. As I grew, I learned compassion and the understanding that life is not always fair. As a teenager, I grew determined and proud, seasoned in many ways with the unique blessings in my path, determined to see it through, to prove them wrong and to let their evil bear the shame.

It was the entire journey that taught me life's greatest lesson, and that is to look outside the walls of circumstance and open your heart. Be mindful of those around you for they are there at that very moment for a purpose. Everything happens for a reason, and the greatest healer of all is the love you can give.

Let that be the Moral of My Story.

A special thanks to those who have made a difference in the creation of this work...

Kamela Mirich, Personal Stylist

Nellie Kaniski, Spiritual Advisor

Penny Lucio, Spiritual Advisor

Michael Gould, Wordsmithing

Holly Senecal, Review Copy

Robert Gould, Cover Design

The staff at Bryan Edwards:

Jennifer Miles

Eileen Magadan

Jackie Murr

For their hard work and moral support